Illustrations to Dante's Inferno

Also by Eugene Paul Nassar

Wallace Stevens: An Anatomy of Figuration
The Rape of Cinderella: Essays in Literary Continuity
The Cantos of Ezra Pound: The Lyric Mode
Essays Critical and Metacritical

DANTE

CON L'ESPOSITIONE

DI CHRISTOFORO LANDINO,

ET DI ALESSANDRO VELLVTELLO,

Sopra la sua Comedia dell'Inferno, del Purgatorio, & del Paradiso:

Con tauole, argomenti, & allegorie, & riformato, riueduto,
& ridotto alla sua uera lettura,

PER FRANCESCO SANSOVINO FIORENTINO.

IN VENETIA, Appresso Giouambattista, Marchiò Sessa, & fratelli. 1564

1564 ed., Venice, woodcut.

Illustrations to Dante's Inferno

EUGENE PAUL NASSAR

Rutherford • Madison • Teaneck
Fairleigh Dickinson University Press
London and Toronto: Associated University Presses

Associated University Presses
440 Forsgate Drive
Cranbury, NJ 08512

Associated University Presses
25 Sicilian Avenue
London WC1A 2QH, England

Associated University Presses
P.O. Box 338, Port Credit
Mississauga, Ontario
Canada L5G 4L8

The paper used in this publication meets the requirements
of the American National Standard for Permanence of Paper
for Printed Library Materials Z39.48-1984.

Library of Congress Cataloging-in-Publication Data

Nassar, Eugene Paul.
    Illustrations to Dante's Inferno / Eugene Paul Nassar.
        p.   cm.
    Includes bibliographical references and index.
    ISBN 0-8386-3426-5
    1. Dante Alighieri, 1265–1321.   Inferno—Illustrations.   2. Hell
in art.   I. Title.
PQ4329.N37   1994
741.6′4′0945—dc20   90-56173
                                                              CIP

PRINTED IN THE UNITED STATES OF AMERICA

To Mr. Thomas Yoseloff:
Publisher, Author, Connoisseur—
For His Many Kindnesses
Over the Past Twenty-Seven Years

Contents

Acknowledgments	8
Preface	9
Introduction	11
Notes to the Plates	28
Plates	30
Select List of Illustrated Editions	388
Select Bibliography	391
Index	396

Acknowledgments

Ln A BOOK SUCH AS THIS WITH OVER FOUR-HUNDRED PLATES, IT IS IMPOSSIBLE TO GIVE FULL citation here regarding any specific plate. The caption to each plate and the Index citation for a given institution will often supply information not here included. Acknowledged below is, variously, ownership of an art work, holder of a copyright, the supply of and/or permission to use a given plate. (The great majority of the plates have come from three sources: The Pontifical Institute of Toronto, Canada, which made available to me the plates used in the Bollingen edition of the illuminated manuscripts [Princeton University Press, 1969]; Art Resource/Alinari of New York; The Cornell University Rare Book Department and the Cornell Photo Lab.)

Biblioteca Angelica (Rome)
Biblioteca Apostolica Vaticana
Biblioteca Comunale (Imola)
Biblioteca Estense (Modena)
BIblioteca Girolamini (Naples)
Biblioteca Laurenziana (Florence)
Biblioteca Marciana (Venice)
Biblioteca Nazionale (Florence)
Biblioteca Riccardiana (Florence)
Biblioteca del Seminario (Padua)
Bibliothèque Nationale (Paris)
Birmingham Art Gallery (England)
British Museum and Library (London)
Leonard Baskin
Centro Dantesco (Ravenna, Aldo Greco, and Michael Mesaros)
Robert Cimbalo
Constance Lebrun Crown
Fogg Museum (Harvard University); *bequest of Grenville L. Winthrop*
G.E.C. Gad Publishers (Copenhagan, Denmark; pub. Ebba Holm, 1929)
Kunsthaus Zurich (paintings of Henry Fuseli)
Manchester City Art Gallery (England, painting of George Watt)

The Pierpont Morgan Library, New York
Musée Condé, Chantilly, France
Musée Rodin, Paris
National Gallery of Victoria (Melbourne, Australia, Blake drawings); *Felton Bequest, 1920*
Oeffentliche Kunstsammlung Basel, Kunstmuseum (painting by Kokoschka)
Ordrupgaard Collection, Copenhagan, Denmark (Delacroix's *Ugolino*)
Pinacoteca di Siena (Giovanni di Paolo)
Schack Galerie, Munich (Feuerbach painting)
SIAE, Italy
Kupferstichkabinett, Staatliche Museen, Preussischer Kulturbesitz, Berlin (Botticelli drawings)
Tate Gallery, London (Blake, Rossetti)
Gabinetto Disegni e Stampe degli Uffizi, Florence (Zuccaro)
University Library, Budapest
VAGA, New York City
Trustees of the Wallace Collection, London (Scheffer painting)

8

Preface

THIS VOLUME IS INTENDED PRIMARILY TO FILL A NEED LONG FELT BY ME AND, I WOULD PRESUME, by thousands of teachers like me who are year after year having their students read Dante's *Inferno* in translation in the survey course of world literature. The student is almost always fascinated by, in addition to other magnificent virtues in the *Inferno*, Dante's overpowering visual imagination. The desire is, then, to search for the illustrative material directly treating, or at least indirectly influenced by, the *Inferno*. But it is a search that can be carried on with some comprehensiveness only in the largest libraries in America and then often only in the rare book rooms of these libraries. There have, to be sure, been published in the last twenty-five years, in conjunction with the 700th anniversary of Dante's birth in 1265, several magnificent volumes dealing with illustrations to the *Divine Comedy*, though often these are foreign-language editions and are rarely found on American library shelves. And, in general, even these volumes are both expensive and specialized, dealing with specific time periods, such as the miniatures in the illuminated manuscripts of the fourteenth and fifteenth centuries, the earliest printed editions of the fifteenth and sixteenth, or the illustrations of a single artist, such as Botticelli, Signorelli, or Blake.

The purpose of this volume is to offer to a wide general public, and in a relatively inexpensive and compact format, a critical overview of illustrations to the *Inferno* from the age of Dante to modern times.

I have selected in the more than 400 plates in this volume what seem to me the finest *Inferno* illustrations from the many thousands of possibilities, as I have reviewed them in the great Dante Collection in the Rare Book Department at Cornell University. I am neither professional Dante scholar nor art historian. My criteria of selection are those of a literary critic seeking fidelity to the tone and texture of a literary masterpiece. My Introduction to follow will argue these criteria. I have organized the selections in a canto-by-canto format, which should prove convenient for both the teacher and student and allow for comparative studies. In matters of Dante's text, I have generally been guided by the translations, notes, and commentary of the Carlyle-Wicksteed, Ciardi, Musa, and Singleton editions.

Whatever merits this volume may have as literary and illustration criticism, its obligations to the wide and elegant world of Dante scholarship, bibliography, and iconography will be obvious. My Introduction, Notes, and Bibliography will enumerate these obligations, but I must here acknowledge with pleasure more specific obligations. Librarians have always been close to my heart, and especially so with this study. James Tyler at the Rare Book Department at Cornell, Pat Dugan, Jill Bergmann, Amy Lopez, Elizabeth Pattengill, Pat Burchard, Rosemary Anguish, and Karen Hansel at the Library of Utica College, Frank Dugan at the Colgate University Library, and Frank Lorenz at the Hamilton College Library, have all shown kindness to me beyond any call to duty. Donald Koetp at the Princeton University Library was kind enough to lend me a book unavailable at any other library in the country. Prof. James Powell of the Department of History at Syracuse University answered many questions of mine with patience. Father Findley of the Pontifical Institute of Toronto, Canada, was most kind, as was Thomas Yoseloff, who encouraged this project from the beginning, as he had already done with two previous books of mine. Professor David Erdman and William Coakley of the *Bulletin of Research in the Humanities* accepted a shortened and revised version of my Introduction, together with nineteen plates, and saw through the press a beautifully printed article in the farewell issue (87:4). An article I developed from my "Notes to the Special Section" entitled "The Iconography of Hell," with twenty-eight plates, is in *Dante Studies*, vol. CXI (1993). My friend and colleague, Robert Cimbalo, whose Dante *Inferno* illustrations have had wide recent exhibition, gave me invaluable counsel in every visual aspect of this study. Barry De Libero at Cornell photographed all the book editions with great artistry and attention to detail, aided by Lucy Burgess of the Cornell Rare Book Department. John Ricco of Art Resource was very kind in his efforts to secure photographs for me, as was Alessandra de Angelis Flint in aiding me with bibliographic translation. Julien Yoseloff, Michael Koy, Rebecca Woolston, and Caterina Mercone of Associated University Presses have edited the manuscript with great patience and skill.

Finally, I must confess to taking great pleasure in writing this in the home of my birth in the Italian-American neighborhood of East Utica in Upstate New York, and thinking that I might have made some small contribution to the wider enjoyment and appreciation of the greatest of all Italian writers. I think back too to the splendid teachers of my youth who made literature of central importance to my life: Professors John Crowe Ransom and Denham Sutcliffe at Kenyon College, Christopher Ricks at Worcester College, Oxford University, and Arthur Mizener at Cornell University.

Introduction

BERNARD BERENSON, IN AN ESSAY IN *THE NATION* DATED 24 DECEMBER 1893 ENTITLED "DANTE'S Visual Images and His Early Illustrators," issued a call for

> an edition of the *Commedia* with illustrations chosen from the finest of the fourteenth and fifteenth centuries, and from the best by Signorelli and Botticelli, supplemented by such parallel conceptions as may be found in Dante's contemporaries, and even in Michelangelo. . . . The editor of such an edition will find that the ground has been well prepared by Dr. Ludwig Volkmann.

The fourteenth and fifteenth-century illustrations to which Berenson is especially referring are the miniatures in the illuminated manuscripts. A comprehensive edition of these had to wait for the magnificent Bollingen edition, *Illuminated Manuscripts of the Divine Comedy* of 1969 (edited by Peter Brieger, Millard Meiss, and Charles S. Singleton). I share Berenson's delight with the miniatures and indeed fully one-quarter of the selections in this volume are from the miniatures. Dante's contemporaries are also represented here, as are Signorelli, Botticelli, and Michelangelo, and the selections from subsequent artists and illustrators follow largely the scholarship and judgments of Dr. Ludwig Volkmann, as presented in his *Iconographia Dantesca* (English revised edition of 1899).

But I cannot agree with Berenson's view concerning Dante's "visual images":

> Few students of Dante stop to wonder what correspondence there can be between his visual images while writing and those called up in our minds while reading him . . . in a lover of the arts such as Dante was, visualization would be largely determined by the works of art with which he was intimately acquainted. It is Giotto whom Dante knew best and loved best, and it is the study of Giotto, therefore, and of kindred painters (some even closer in spirit to Dante, such as Duccio, Simone Martini, and the Lorenzetti) that will enable us to form a clear conception of Dante's visual images.

I can accept the idea that Dante's experience with the visual arts would condition his visualizations of the scenes and characters he creates in his *Inferno*, but I would not want to go so far with Berenson as to say, for instance, that "Michelangelo's attitude is already quite like our own, and his visual images could give no clue to Dante's." It would seem to me that the prime references in Dante's mind as he was writing and visualizing his *Commedia* would not be the paintings of a Giotto or Duccio, but the men and women of Florence and in general the scenes from life in the hills and valleys of Tuscany. I see no reason, therefore, to suppose that, after a short period of re-orientation, Dante would not have embraced the frescos of Signorelli at Orvieto and of Michelangelo in the Sistine Chapel as equally great if not greater illustrations of his work than the greatest of the miniaturists. For that matter, I can imagine Dante saying much the same about Delacroix's painting, *Dante's Bark* of 1822.

Dante illustration need not be confined to the visualizations of medieval artists any more than Homeric illustration need be confined to renderings of the artists of ancient Greece. Complex, yet sufficiently universal human situations in one cultural context are dramatized by a subtle artist of one time period, and his attitudes toward the situations are sufficiently communicated to the willing and sensitive reader of a different cultural context or another time period. This in large measure is what we mean when we speak of world literature. The good literary critic must be that sensitive reader; so, too, must be the good illustrator. It is of course not enough that the illustrator be a sensitive reader; he must to an equal degree have the artist's eye and hand and spirit. Often in the illustrations to follow there will be lacking either the fidelity to Dante's attitudes or the artistic execution. The greatest illustrations will encompass a mastery of both virtues of the illustrator's art.

First, I would speak of some of the disappointments one will find in these illustrations. The reader, flushed with enthusiasm after reading, say, Canto 10 of the great Farinata degli Uberti, who holds all of Hell in grand despite, and then perhaps Erich Auerbach's subtle appreciation of the Canto in *Mimesis*, will not find any illustration that will come close to the wonderful complexity of the scene. The scene awaits a future Delacroix or Michelangelo. The same can be said for the moving scene of Dante with his beloved teacher Ser Brunetto Latini in Canto 15. There are perhaps explanations for the paucity of good illustrations of the Farinata and Ser Brunatto and other scenes; perhaps in some cases mere chance has ruled. There are also many cases where an artist of major talent turned Dante illustrator is really far more interested in his own personal artistic statements than in Dante's text and tone (his complex attitudes). Such a charge may at times be brought, has been brought, against Botticelli, Blake, and many of Dante's nineteenth- and twentieth-century illustrators.

I have said that fidelity to Dante's text and tone is the necessary though not sufficient requirement for the good illustration to the *Inferno*. But there are those who would question whether there *is* any such thing as an objectively existing tone in Dante, or in any literary work. The question has in fact been virgorously debated in the literary criticism of recent decades concerning contextualism, intertextualism, and deconstruction of texts. My position, as outlined in previous books, is that precision of statement concerning attitudes of an author in his text is attainable as a limit, that is, that there are better and worse readings of a text, and demonstrably so. It is possible to say that no illustrations of the Farinata scene come close to Dante's attitudes, though some come closer than others. It is possible to say that Blake's Capaneus (from Canto 14), while a great drawing in itself, is far more Blake's than Dante's, and that the miniaturists' Capaneus of Vat. MS 4776 and B.N. MS it 74 are far closer to Dante's, and, on balance, better illustration to Dante.

I remember vividly the experience of first reading Dante in the mid-1950s at Kenyon College. We were using the stimulating translation of the *Inferno* of John Ciardi, which had recently appeared, and the required readings on the reserve shelf were the essays of George Santayana in *Three Philosophic Poets* (ca. 1910), T. S. Eliot in *The Sacred Wood* (1920), and Erich Auerbach in *Mimesis* (1953), whose essay had appeared earlier in the *Kenyon Review*. These essays still seem to be paradigmatic in defining the literary consciousness of the *Inferno* in the English-speaking world, and I want to refer to them in attempting to articulate my sense of the tone of the work.

Dante is one of the supreme dramatists of the human condition; this needs to be emphasized more than his Aristotelean or Aquinian, his classical or medieval roots. Auerbach is more right in speaking of Dante's "tensely dramatic relationship to his own work" than Santayana of Dante's "prophetic absoluteness." Santayana, for all of the occasional acuteness of analysis in his essay, wants to see Dante as a philosopher first and poet second:

> Dante was far from perfect, even as a poet. He was too much a man of his own time, and often wrote with a passion not clarified into judgement. . . . We feel too much, in these cases, the heat of the poet's prejudice or indignation. He is not just, as he usually is; he does not stop to think, as he almost always does. He forgets that he is in the eternal world, and dips for the moment into a brawl in some Italian market-place, or into the council-chamber of some factious *condottiere*. . . .
>
> Moreover, the personality thrust forward so obtrusively is not in every respect worthy of contemplation. Dante is very proud and very bitter; at the same time, he is curiously timid; and one may tire sometimes of his perpetual tremblings and tears, of his fainting fits and his intricate doubts. A man who knows he is under the special protection of God, and of three celestial ladies, and who has such a sage and magician as Virgil for a guide, might have looked upon hell with a little more confidence.

Contrast Auerbach's view of essentially the same effects in the *Inferno:*

> Never before has this realism been carried so far; never before—scarcely even in antiquity—has so much art and so much expressive power been employed to produce an almost painfully immediate impression of the earthly reality of human beings. . . .
>
> We experience an emotion which is concerned with human beings and not directly with the divine order in which they have found their fulfillment. Their eternal position in the divine order is something of which we are only conscious as a setting whose irrevocability can but serve to heighten the effect of their humanity, preserved for us in all its force. The result is a direct experience of life which overwhelms everything else, a comprehension of human realities which spreads as widely and variously as it goes profoundly to the very roots of our emotions, an illumination of man's impulses and passions which leads us to share in them without restraint and indeed to admire their variety and their greatness.

Santayana finds Dante's passions and intricate doubts disconcerting; Auerbach finds them admirable. T. S. Eliot, and much of the modern literary criticism which he in large measure established, agrees with Auerbach in seeing this complexity of tone, this ambivalence, as an artistic virtue. I would not only agree, but would assert that Dante consciously dramatized his intricate doubts to give full expression (to use romantic terminology) to his soul.

Dante, a man of faith but also of intricate doubts, is profoundly moved and baffled (and remains so) by Virgil's fate, condemned to Limbo, profoundly moved with compassion for Paolo and Francesca's fate, for Pier delle Vigne, for Jacopo Rusticucci, for Ugolino, even for Jason, Ulysses, and Brutus. Their fates of course *must* be just, for God is a God of Justice and of Love, but Dante consistently suspends judgment of the sinner's sin and weeps for his fate.

Dante is, in fact, profoundly Italian and Mediterranean in this suspension of judgment and in so many other aspects of his mind and art. He delights in paying off old scores, as with Filippo Argenti; he understands and agrees with the desire of so many of the sinners in Hell to be known and remembered in the world above, even as sinners damned to Hell; he understands and agrees with cousin Geri del Bello's expectation that his family should avenge his murder; he loves the cant and slang of conmen; he delights, much in the tradition of the medieval "flytings," or insult contests (*cf.* in Dante's *Rime*, the poems to and from Forese Donati), in the irrepressible stream of invective he pours over all the important towns of Tuscany and beyond. Dante delights also in the burlesque humor with which he ridicules the usurers of Canto 17, who save places for comrades still alive on earth, the flatterers of Canto 18, who steam in a river of excrement, the grafters of Cantos 21 and 22, which include the whole town of Lucca, the treacherous of Canto 33, where he finds the souls of Fra Alberigo and Branca D'Oria though their bodies still walk the earth. One should not miss the sardonic joy, the Rabelaisian gusto, of Dante having the simoniacs head down in burning holes similar to baptismal fonts, Pope Nicholas awaiting the coming of his two Papal successors, the soul of Guido da Montefeltro being argued over by St. Francis and a devil in scholastic debate. Such grim, wonderful humor is everywhere in the *Inferno*. The picture of Dante at his desk poring over volumes of Aristotle and Aquinas is a two-dimensional Dante. Such a Dante would, upon reaching the deepest pit of Hell, never have the farcical name-calling between the dropsical Mastro Adamo and the smoking Sinon, or the slashing and abusive wit of Bocca degli Abati and Buoso da Duera, or the masterstroke of Satan weeping eternally.

This complexity of tone, this ambivalence, this "tensely dramatic relationship to his own work," the Aquinian faith and the intricate doubts, the compassion and the invective, the sardonic comedy and poignant tragedy, the Mediterraneanness and the universality, are all encompassed in the Dantean text. We look to the artist or illustrator to capture faithfully some aspect of that tonality rather than, as is too often the case, simply to use the Dantean text for the expression of his own outside interests.

The early miniatures in the illuminated manuscripts and the engravings and woodcuts in the early printed editions often exhibit problems of execution, and are often crude, simplistic, or ludicrous as representations of the text. But they are also always interesting and sometimes, at their strongest, remarkably beautiful and expressive of Dante's text. Berenson defers to Volkmann's scholarship in the matter of the miniatures, but insofar as he has studied the extant manuscripts, he chooses four manuscripts from which he would certainly select if the anthology he proposed were to appear: 1) Florence, Biblioteca Nazionale, MS Palat. 313, 2) Venice, Biblioteca Marciana, MS it. IX. 276, 3) Rome, Biblioteca Angelica, MS 1102, 4) Vatican, Biblioteca Apostolica, MS Urb. lat. 365. All of these manuscripts are represented in my selections, but the wider scholarship and the hundreds of plates in the Bollingen edition of 1969 (cited above) have allowed me to select from a much wider field the miniatures that seem to me to come closest to being true illustrations of the *Inferno*. I would note here five manuscripts whose miniatures generally stand out from the rest in interpretive power. They are 1) Chantilly, Musée Conde, MS 597, 2) Vatican, Biblioteca Apostolica, MS lat. 4776, 3) Paris, Bibliothèque Nationale, MS it. 74, 4) Paris, Bibliothèque Nationale, MS it. 2017, 5) London, British Museum, Yates Thompson MS 36.

I call the reader's attention especially to the Vatican MS lat. 4776, from which I have selected thirty-five plates, more than twice the number from any other manuscript. The artist of Vat. 4776 is concerned always with the appropriateness of facial expression and body gesture to the situation Dante is describing. The Avaricious

(Canto 7) endlessly rolling rocks (as in life minding their wealth) are all pained by their labor, but each differently. That this is intentionally done is clear in the preparatory drawing, especially in the two figures at the lower left. The Capaneus of Vat. 4776 (Canto 14) is quite right, lying in an attitude of proud and sullen insolence, in direct contrast to the suffering about him. And also in contrast to the Capaneus of William Blake, who clearly represents something radiant and heroic in the human spirit, Blake's Capaneus, not Dante's. I can only agree with Professor Peter Brieger when he says in the Bollingen edition that Vat. 4776 is "important and much too little known."

With the depiction of the scene of the Hypocrites in the two manuscripts in the Bibliothèque Nationale in Paris (Canto 23 and the Special Section), we are at the level of high art and high illustration, unsurpassed down through the centuries, despite the popularity of the scene with illustrators. To compare with the Chantilly depiction of the Lukewarm of Canto 3, we have only Signorelli's fresco in the cathedral at Orvieto (Spec. Sec.) that can match it in energy and grace. The Brunetto Latini of the Yates Thompson MS (Canto 15) is one of the very few where the subtle, dramatic, and highly moving interview between Dante and Ser Brunetto is caught with any adequacy.

The Vatican MS Urb. lat. 365, represented here by ten plates, is highly praised by Berenson as the "most valuable" of later manuscripts, and by Volkmann as a work which "stands alone of its kind." It is indeed everywhere artistically beautiful, having come late enough (1478) to be influenced by Pier della Francesca, but it cannot be considered so highly as illustration to Dante. The tonality of these miniatures has been articulated by Professor Brieger as

> the transformation of the frightening subterranean Hell into an Elysium, the beauty of which is marred only slightly by the afflictions suffered by the handsome nudes carefully disposed on a deep stage beneath the open sky.

The drawings of Sandro Botticelli for Dante's *Commedia*, contemporary with the Vat. 365 manuscript, have drawn from Bernard Berenson much the same sort of critique as the Vatican manuscript from Brieger:

> To many these illustrations will be disappointing. They have heard that Botticelli was a great artist, and they expect him to give them, to an even intenser degree, feelings of the kind and quality that they have had in reading Dante. . . . Botticelli was not the man for the task. . . . Their value consists in their being drawings by Botticelli, not at all in their being drawings for Dante. . . . I will not deny that in many of those [drawings] for the "Inferno" there is somewhat more correspondence with the text, but I doubt whether it is ever enough to be satisfactory as expression, while it is precisely in such drawings that the artist is least satisfactory as pure art.

Berenson is reviewing Professor F. Lippmann's splendid 1896 English edition of the Botticelli drawings (*The Nation*, 12 November, 1896), calling it "one of the great events of recent years" and Botticelli "the greatest master of the single line that our modern Western world has yet possessed." Professor Lippmann (whose photographs of the drawings are here reproduced) has a much higher opinion of the drawings as Dante illustration:

> rising immeasurably above all kindred works, it became one of the most significant artistic renderings ever given to poetry, and not the least among the many marvels of the Italian Renaissance.

Volkmann has a similar opinion:

no other artist of the Renaissance was so well fitted for the work of illustrating the "Divine Comedy" as Sandro Botticelli.

As does the recent editor of the drawings, Sir Kenneth Clark:

> In face of such drawings as these, it is hard to believe that anyone could say that Botticelli fails as an illustrator, even in those parts of the *Divine Comedy* that would seem to be least suited to his genius.

I can only encourage the reader to peruse every corner of each of Botticelli's illustrations with the text of the *Inferno* in hand. There are marvelous vignettes everywhere in the details of the drawings, an obviously powerful mind and spirit in the artist interpreting the text. There are also other details of expression and gesture that seem merely perfunctory. (The drawings are meant to be read as flowing narrative, Dante and Virgil appearing more than once in the same drawing as they move through sequences of the *Inferno*.) I would suggest that these drawings, at least initially, were conceived by Botticelli as preliminary for what were to be finished small paintings, where all details of expression and gesture would be refined. Four of the drawings, in fact, are colored; some of the drawings are clearly more finished than others. Professor Lippmann traces the many starts and stops in Botticelli's work on the drawings during his lifetime. The project was clearly important to Botticelli, but, for whatever reasons, uncompleted. Many of Berenson's objections to the *Inferno* drawings as illustration can be traced, I think, to their unfinished state. But, one must admit, not all. There is, perhaps, some fundamental hesitation in Botticelli's nature concerning the punishments in the *Inferno;* the *Paradiso* is more congenial to his spirit.

With the Vatican MS Urb lat. 365 manuscript and the Botticelli drawings, we are at the end of the era of the illuminated manuscript and the beginning of the era of the printed book. Botticelli's drawings, the first nineteen of them, we assume with Botticelli's agreement, are the basis for an illustrated Florentine edition of 1481, using copperplate engravings. Nine of these are reproduced in this volume. Volkmann, Lippmann, Berenson, and Clark all have a low opinion of these engravings. I find them to have a good deal of merit and expressive power, derived no doubt in large measure from their use of the Botticelli drawings. It seems they have suffered in critical estimation both from comparison with their source and also from their being, in turn, the source for the quite inferior woodcuts of subsequent printed editions by various publishers in 1487, 1491, 1493, 1497, and on into the sixteenth century. I have included only one plate (Canto 7) from the late-fifteenth-century editions, which illustrations Berenson labels as "infantile," Lippmann as "mean," and A. W. Pollard, in his *Early Illustrated Books,* as "coarsely executed" and "of no merit." In turning the pages of these editions, the reader will find that the illustrations at times have some charm and always some historical interest, but any recollection of Dante's text would cause him to close the books.

The sixteenth-century illustrated printed editions are in general only slight improvements on the late-fifteenth-century editions, from which they are derived. I have perused them all at the Cornell Dante Collection (a dreary business), but have included, save for one important exception, only one plate each from editions of 1506 (Canto 1) and 1555 (Canto 34). The exception is the Venetian edition of 1544. The illustrations in this edition are perhaps not so much illustrations as diagrams, but ingenious and often highly dramatic. They are envisioned by the anonymous designer as horizontal sections of Hell, as Dante and Virgil move ever lower, spiraling downward into circles of ever-decreasing diameter. They are, it seems to me, remarkably effective in creating a sense of claustrophobia and at the same time a sense of Dante's awe at the divine architecture of Hell. These woodcuts are the product of an original and interesting mind, and I have used his designs as canto dividers (using a later 1564 edition); in Canto 8 I have placed a number of them together so that the reader might sense the designer's conception of a continuous sequence of frames.

Meaningful book illustration to the *Inferno* is now dormant for two hundred years, till the Venetian edition of 1757, when interest in Dante was reawakened in Italy. But before moving to the book illustrations of the eighteenth century, we must backtrack to consider illustrative works outside of the manuscript or book which are related in some way to the *Inferno*.

It is beyond the scope of this book to cover the visualizations of Hell of artists preceding Dante, even if the field were restricted to Italy alone. I have made one or two obvious exceptions, however. I include a detail of the mosaic ceiling in the Baptistery in Florence (Spec. Sec.), which was certainly known by Dante and which perhaps can stand as a traditional representation of Hell and Satan in Dante's time. Giotto's representation of Hell and Satan (Spec. Sec.) in the Arena Chapel in Padua is, in fact, closer to the Baptistery representation than to Dante's. The fresco was completed before the writing of the *Commedia*. There is some documentation of friendship and admiration between these two great artists, and it is, therefore, quite possible that both were influenced by the other's conceptions. Volkmann notes that both Vasari and Benvenuto da Imola testify that Giotto was influenced by Dante. His analysis of the Paduan fresco, however, leads him to assert (and I must agree) that the two artists drew on and developed a common body of ideas (with Dante more bold in breaking with traditional conceptions), that the fresco is certainly not a "hard and fast representation of the poet's Hell," and that the visual correspondences to (or "reminiscences of") Dante's imagery are insufficiently numerous and largely superficial.

Volkmann says much the same about the relationship of the *Inferno* to other frescos or wall panels of the "Last Judgment" or "Hell" by Italian painters of the fourteenth and fifteenth centuries (all in the Special Section): in the Camposanto of Pisa (F. Traini, 1350s), in San Petronio in Bologna (G. da Modena, 1410), in the Duomo in San Gimignano (T. Bartolo, 1393), in the Museo San Marco in Florence (Fra Angelico, 1430s), and in the Academy in Siena (G. di Paolo, 1453). I think Volkmann's position is fair. These are not, as a whole, illustrative of Dante's *Inferno* but are often (as one would expect) influenced by Dante's poem; some details can be considered as illustrative of the *Inferno*. And magnificent details they are, the punishments of Hell done with a zest and, often, a sardonic humor that Dante would have appreciated, and which he himself exhibited over and again in the *Inferno*.

It is to the great fresco by Nardo di Cione in the Strozzi Chapel of Santa Maria Novella in Florence (1350s, Spec. Sec.) that we must go for comprehensive, intentional and magnificent illustrations of the *Inferno*. Whatever the fresco's possible failings as a whole composition, its details deserve a volume of their own. In more than thirty vignettes which make up the whole, Nardo compresses into crowded symbolic space much of the imagery of the *Inferno* as well as much of the tonality: humor, anger, violence, bewilderment, tragedy, and acceptance—an astonishing *tour de force*. Nardo's Avaricious (Canto 7) are, humorously, as in Dante, all clerics, naked save for their hieratical hats and, in two cases, capes, watched over by a pack of devils. The whole has the seriocomic tone so often found in Dante, though often neglected in the Dante criticism. The illustration of Canto 13 has a sense of tragic timelessness, an eerie stasis: the Harpies ever hovering, the suicides ever immobile as brittle sticks, the two squanderers ever pursued by hounds. There is here and everywhere in the Nardo fresco a mastery of the complex, an understanding of, and sympathy for, the full range of Dantean attitudes. The fresco was most influential on subsequent illustration to the *Inferno*. Professors Brieger and Meiss cite Nardo's fresco as the clear inspiration for the Florentine illuminated manuscript Vatican MS lat. 4776, and it was Professor Volkmann who first pointed to the obvious use of Nardo's fresco in the frontispiece of the Florentine illuminated manuscript by Bartolomeo di Fruosino (Paris, B.N. MS it. 74, ca. 1420, Spec. Sec.).

Nardo's fresco is matched in vigor and interpretive power by those of Luca Signorelli in the cathedral of Orvieto done a century and a half later (ca. 1499–1504). Only one fresco, however, has direct relationship to a scene in the *Inferno*: that of the Lukewarm who are stung by wasps as they pursue a wavering banner, while Charon ferries the damned across the river Acheron to be judged on the other shore by Minos (Spec. Sec.). The Charon-Minos scene is also the one scene in the Last Judgment fresco of Michelangelo in the Sistine Chapel (ca. 1540, Spec. Sec.) directly related to Dante's poem. In the Michelangelo, Charon whacks the sinners with his oar just as Dante describes, while Minos, in both the Signorelli and Michelangelo, winds his tail around his body to designate the given sinner's place in Hell, again according to Dante's description.

The two frescos are related in other ways. The evidence is that Michelangelo studied Signorelli's frescos at Orvieto and that both frescos are the products of life-long devotion to Dante and his *Commedia*. (Michelangelo especially, in his reported conversations, his prose, and poetry, and in his [alleged] complete series of drawings to the *Commedia*, lost at sea). Superficially, one can separate these frescos of Signorelli and Michelangelo from Dante's time by focusing on the obvious interest in the nude form and the new Humanism it implies, or on Michelangelo giving the head of a personal enemy to Minos and the awakening of the egoistic personality in art that it implies. But the connection to Dante runs deeper than these stylistic matters in the frescos. A profound Dantean sense of the human condition is depicted in these powerful rhythms of dramatic action and gesture. The tonalities of the Dantean text, the complexity, compassion, the faith and doubt, the sardonic comedy and poignant tragedy have never been so awesomely caught as in these masterful frescos of the sixteenth century.

A century after Botticelli began his series of drawings for the *Commedia*, two journeymen artists in Florence were preparing their own series (ca. 1586–88), which, like Botticelli's, remained unpublished and largely unstudied till the late nineteenth century. The drawings of Frederico Zuccaro are in the Uffizi, and those of Hans van der Straet (a Fleming from Bruges), called Stradanus, are in the Biblioteca Laurenziana in Florence. I have included seven drawings of Zuccaro and eight of Stradanus. Neither can be considered major artists, or illustrators for that matter; they are both too willing too often to give Dante's text only the most perfunctory and banal handling for the most obvious theatrical effects. Both, however, as might be expected of prolific artist-jobbers of the late Italian Renaissance, are capable draughtsmen in a time of high standards, so that one can find at times excellent details in drawing and even of expression and mood in some of the drawings of either man. Stradanus occasionally (Canto 4) is able to evoke an elegiac mood, of the pathos of Hell and of the sinners' suffering, which seems both a personal expression and true to an aspect of Dante's tonality. Zuccaro, often mannered, grotesque, and burlesque, can still at times be very moving, as with the giants of Canto 31, the powerful bodies powerless and straining in endless confinement.

As mentioned earlier, the seventeenth and the first half of the eighteenth centuries saw a slackening of interest in Dante, with very few new editions of the text. No illustrations worthy of comment appear till the Venetian edition of 1757, which, for all the magnificence of the edition, is not distinguished in its copper engravings by various hands. The few that I have selected (Cantos 4, 8, 20, 24), from three different artists, are, of course, those that I feel come closest to Dante's text, but they share with all of the plates of the 1757 edition a landscape of Hell which is rather serene and placid, an ordered place, punctuated here and there with the grotesqueries of the punishments of sinners, rather like a Sunday stroll through a giant outdoor zoological park. It is an eighteenth century Age-of-Reason Hell, not Dante's, but ever so often, as in the selected pieces, we find an artist at least temporarily interested in the psychological state of the sinners or their impact on Dante and Virgil.

Interest in Dante spread at a phenomenal rate in the last half of the eighteenth century all over the European continent and England, and to America and the rest of the world in the nineteenth and twentieth centuries.

Henry Fuseli, a Swiss who became a naturalized Englishman, was doing vivid sketches from Dante as early as 1774 (Canto 32). Paget Toynbee, in an essay on "The Earliest English Illustrators of Dante," discusses Sir Joshua Reynolds's *Ugolino and His Sons* (1773) as the first "easel picture" ever done on a Dante theme. It is the first in a long line of paintings and sculpture of the Ugolino scene of Canto 33 throughout the nineteenth century, of which should be mentioned especially those of the French Romantic artists Gericault, Delacroix, and the sculptor Rodin. The popularity of the Ugolino scene is surpassed only by the fantastic profusion of paintings and sculpture on the Paolo and Francesca theme of Canto 5 (see the comprehensive book on the subject by Guglielmo Locella in 1913), of which are included here those of Shaeffer, Rossetti, Watts, Feuerbach, Rodin, and Kokoschka. Added to this list must be the great number of nineteenth-century paintings of scenes from Dante's life and thought and his relationship with Beatrice, as in the works of Dante Gabriel Rossetti and Anselm Feuerbach. This flood of impressionistic derivations from one romantic and one pathetic scene in the *Inferno*, and from Dante's life as outlined in the *Vita Nuova*, lies beyond the scope of this book. It is to work truly meant to be illustrative of the *Inferno* that we must give major attention.

The nineteenth century saw a great number of illustrated editions of the *Commedia* in many languages, many of them large, beautifully printed, multi-volumed productions. I have perused these editions in the Cornell Dante Collection. I have not selected any plates from a number of them (I note some of them in my Bibliography). Their absence is, of course, my only comment on them as illustrations to the *Inferno*. Most influential are John Flaxman's illustrations to the *Commedia* printed in Italy in 1793. I have included seventeen of Flaxman's plates, more than I would have strictly on their merits in catching Dante's tone, but they were so highly praised and copied by artists of the early nineteenth century, so highly reproduced throughout that century, and yet so rarely seen in this century, that their historical importance alone warrants the number included here. Flaxman (like Fuseli, a lifelong friend of William Blake) was praised and studied for the abstracting simplicity and economy of line in these Dante illustrations by artists of the caliber of Ingres, David, Gericault, and Goya. The illustrations seem to me often admirable in design; whatever passion they elicit, however, is rarely conveyed by the expressions on the faces of the participants. The Virgil and Dante figures in general have reactions ranging from impassive to banal to insipid. The illustrator seems rarely moved or genuinely involved with the text and its complexities. These faults are accentuated in illustrators imitative of Flaxman such as Macchiavelli and Genelli. Flaxman's clearest successes are in the illustration of Canto 23, Caiaphas and the Hypocrites (where Virgil and Dante do not even appear) and of Canto 31, where the giant is admirably drawn, though he seems to be protecting the pair rather than (as in Dante's text) grudgingly conveying them to the pit of Hell.

In Germany, Joseph Anton Koch was a prolific and often effective illustrator of the *Commedia* from the earliest years of the nineteenth century, although most of the illustrations remained unpublished till a selection of them was made for an Italian edition in 1904. Koch's compositions are inspired by Classicism and Early and Renaissance Italian art, and while often both landscape and figure are lovely, there is usually a placidity or even blandness in his Dante renditions; his Harpies of Canto 13 are more cherubic than ghastly, the Flatterers of Canto 18 have perhaps more charm than loathsomeness. A fresco of Dante and Virgil decending to the lower Hell on the back of Geryon (Canto 17) has, however, fine expressiveness in the faces. The Brunelleschi of Canto 25 is Koch's greatest success in the powerful depiction of the dragon at Brunelleschi's neck.

In Italy the sumptuous 1817 Ancora edition has drawings to the *Inferno* by Luigi Ademolli which proved to be very popular in Italy and Europe throughout the nineteenth century. I find many of Ademolli's drawings both charming and close to aspects of Dante's tonality. (I am puzzled therefore to find Ludwig Volkmann rather vehement in his dislike of Ademolli's work.) I think Dante would have been pleased with the Botticellian beauty of Ademolli's Beatrice (Canto 2) and his Francesca (Canto 5). The slime of the Gluttons (Canto 6) is well depicted, Ciacco among the other hoggish. The suicide Pier delle Vigne is well caught in a moment of agony, as a branch is broken that he might speak (Canto 13). There is a touch of burlesque humor in the *malebolge* (Canto 21), which is faithful to the poet's text. The snake-horror (Canto 25) is much like Koch's, save that the metamorphosis of man-into-snake is caught halfway in the process, an effect closely described in Dante but not handled since the early Chantilly manuscript.

Bartolomeo Pinelli's *invenzioni* on the *Commedia* of 1826 are highly theatrical, both in the strongly emphasized and dramatized Dante and Virgil figures, and also in the gestures of the various sinners: Charon's angry and arrogant pose of Canto 3, the turned-away shame of Paolo and Francesca of Canto 5, the eagerness to be heard of Ulysses of Canto 26. Verve and pathos are Pinelli's strengths; a tendency towards melodrama his weakness.

Delacroix's *Dante's Bark* is certainly the most famous, perhaps the best, easel painting ever done on a Dantean theme (Spec. Sec.). His friend and patron, Gericault, had done an Ugolino painting in 1815, perhaps stimulating the young Delacroix. Delacroix's painting stunned the Parisian world in 1822 and has been widely admired and studied ever since. It is a true illustration, quite close in both action and tone to the Dantean text; indeed Delacroix, like Michelangelo inspired throughout his life by Dante, notes that he had a friend recite Canto 8 in Italian to him as he painted the work. The painting recalls both Michelangelo and Gericault. Its treatment of the doomed in the water is brilliant and varied; their execution must have stirred some deep feelings of both terror and compassion in Delacroix, conveying a sense of life as poignant tragedy that accords with the ground bass in Dante's works and perhaps accounts in some measure for Delacroix's veneration of the poet.

The more than one hundred drawings of William Blake to the *Commedia* (seventy-two to the *Inferno*) were done in the last years of Blake's life (1824–27). Most are unfinished, some merely pencil sketches, some tinted with watercolors. Seven engravings of drawings were also completed by Blake. As any student of Blake's illustrations of other literary works would expect, these are part illustration of Dante, part debate with Dante. I have, in the thirty-two plates I have selected from Blake, chosen, of course, those that best illustrate Dante's text rather than Blake's concepts, those that need no special knowledge of Blake's system of ideas. The plates here included seem to me most striking and original, and obviously derived from a powerful imagination. Blake's Capaneus (Canto 14), his Vanni Fucci (Canto 25), and his giants (Canto 31), are all quite different from Dante's, as they are fighting Dante's God, Blake's Nobodaddy, and so are admirable to Blake. It is as the first editor of these drawings, Albert Roe, says, "The entire fabric of Dante's poem must . . . in Blake's opinion have been built upon a fundamental error." But it is also, as Roe further says, "As to his opinion of him [Dante] as an artist, there can be no doubt that Blake considered him in the highest category." It is furthermore clear to this writer that no matter how disaffected intellectually Blake may have been with Dante's Hell of punishment and retribution, he is fascinated with it and creates over and again in designs of great intensity and dynamism, sinners being bitten by snakes, swirled in the wind, chased by dogs, hacked by devils, and locked in ice. The drawings are in large measure defined by this fascination. The case is perhaps, as Blake thought it was with Milton, that Blake is, to a large extent, of Dante's party without knowing it. To a large enough extent, in any case, to capture often in his drawings a Dantean scene with Dantean force.

Dante Gabriel Rossetti and the Pre-Raphaelite Brotherhood were deeply influenced not by the force of the Dante of the *Inferno* but by the Dante of the *Vita Nuova*, the worship of Beatrice and the *donna ideale*. Of Rossetti's many paintings with Dantean themes I therefore reproduce only the *Paolo and Francesca*, which, for all its romantic charm, hardly catches the complex tone of Canto 5. George Watts's painting comes closer, Oscar Kokoschka's even closer. With the Kokoschka painting, we have the Dantean theme used for enormously powerful personal expression. The case is the same with the *Paolo and Francesca* of Rodin.

Among the other Pre-Raphaelites, Burne-Jones has a lovely head of a Beatrice, and Walter Crane a few woodcuts (Canto 1) illustrative of the *Inferno*. Anselm Feuerbach in Germany (Canto 5) seems to me the most gifted of all of the later nineteenth-century painters devoted to Dante (though not to the illustration of the *Inferno*).

But to return to nineteenth-century illustrated editions. In 1861 there appeared in Paris, *L'Enfer, avec les dessins de G. Doré*, certainly the most popular series of illustrations to the *Inferno* of all editions before or since. It has had the highest praise (Gautier, Dumas, Rodin), been criticized by others (Yeats and Berenson), but it is still popular now, 130 years after its appearance, and I think justly so. It is simply the most faithful extended translation of Dante's imagery, atmosphere, and, to a more limited extent, his psychological subtlety, to a visual medium that we have. Doré was a prodigious worker and an enormously talented illustrator, with tremendous empathy for great narrative. He illustrated at a very high level Rabelais, Cervantes, LaFontaine, Perrault, Balzac and hundreds of others, and made wonderful sketches of the streets and people of Paris and London.

His *Inferno* is perhaps his masterpiece. He supervised every detail in the preparation of the engravings, which introduced a technique of tonal shading to gain the resonant chiaroscuro for which the plates are famous. He created, as Nigel Gosling says, ". . . a totally new landscape of the mind, a rocky, precipitous terrain as barren as the moon, at the same time claustrophobic and vertiginous." Doré's vast, grand, and ubiquitous landscapes do indeed add a new dimension to Dante illustration, a dimension perhaps in Dante's mind as he wrote, but not in the visual vocabulary of the artists and illustrators of his time. Berenson, in his essay on "Dante's Visual Images," takes as his premise that Dante would visualize his *Inferno* in images similar to the landscapes of contemporary artists, and that therefore Doré's landscapes get "in the way." I would counter that a writer's visualizations would first proceed from the world as it appears from his window, then perhaps from the way a contemporary artist renders it. I cannot imagine Dante finally preferring the visual images of, say, the Marciana manuscript to those of Signorelli, Michelangelo, Delacroix, or, to be sure, Doré.

Doré's limbo of the great poets of Canto 4 is closer to Dante's description than any other. So with Doré's awful wood of pain of the Suicides of Canto 13; Doré's Harpies there and his Geryon of Canto 17 are not ludicrous as they are not ludicrous to Dante, but are in most of the illustrations to the *Inferno*. Doré's endless march of the Hypocrites (Canto 23) is in a class with Fruosino's, and his evocation of Ulysses speaking from the flame (Canto 26) is the only illustration I have seen that conveys the awe which the scene evokes. Doré is often astonishingly inventive in ways to convey Dante truthfully; he can also at times be flat, overinflated, uninspired, in Yeats's terms, "noisy and demogogic." But he has been and remains the benchmark for all book illustration of the *Inferno*. Rodin has a drawing in the front pages of an *Inferno* illustrated by Doré and the inscription in French "In homage of admiration to a great artist, Gustave Doré, too much forgotten, August Rodin, 1908." It would have meant a great deal to Doré.

Doré was not soon forgotten as the number of new editions of his illustrations attest, as do imitations and borrowings by subsequent illustrators. In 1879 appeared a *Commedia* in French, illustrated by Yan Dargent, obviously deeply indebted to Doré and never as good. The landscape to Canto 11 is evocative, the plate of Caiaphas and the Hypocrites (Canto 23) has a rude power, his Satan (Canto 34) is similarly coarse, but, in catching the detail of the tears, moving. The sardonic poignancy of the fight of the devil and St. Francis over the soul of Guido da Montrefeltro (Canto 27) is effective, and the melange of snakes (Canto 24) is a fine composition.

A greater disciple of Doré's is Manfredo Manfredini in an Italian edition of 1907. Manfredini's landscapes (Cantos 1, 4, 7, 11, 18) are at times even more vast, grand, and ubiquitous than Doré's, symbolically right for Dante's sense of the perilousness of human choice and judgment. Manfredini's Paolo is interesting in his clutching to Francesca rather than, as usual, holding her protectively (Canto 5). In general, Manfredini's illustrations deserve to be better known.

A few years after the appearance of Doré's *Inferno*, a large edition of illustrations to the *Commedia* by Francesco Scaramuzza was published sequentially in Parma, Italy (3 vol., 1865–70), and for the next decade there was debate in the periodicals about the relative merits of the Dante illustrations of Doré and Scaramuzza. Time appears to have decided in Doré's favor, but many of the Scaramuzza plates still retain a good deal of charm and vitality. Scaramuzza, director of the Gallery at Parma, shows obvious influence of Signorelli's fresco of Canto 3, but in general Scaramuzza's nudes are rendered too naturalistically. The heads, the gestures, are often as if simply sketched from life at a village piazza or a penal camp (Volkmann is reminded of a "house of correction"). One has a sense in these drawings of a photograph album of nineteenth-century provincial Italian life, a vulgarization of Dante, though the *Inferno* at times certainly has something of the spirit of *Campanilismo* or local particularity. And Dante would have appreciated the comedy in Scaramuzza's depiction of the climbing down (and up) Satan's hairy body out of Hell (Canto 34).

The nineteenth century ends in book illustration with the influence of William Morris and *Art Nouveau* (see Walter Crane, Canto 1, and J. D. Batten, Canto 2), and these influences are clear also in the drawings of Franz Stassen in a German edition of 1906 (Cantos 2 and 25). Essentially decorative, they rarely capture a complex Dantean tonality. The scenes of the *Inferno* are paraded, often with delightful line, but with little of Dante's inner life: the common malaise of book illustration in general.

The twentieth century (as the nineteenth) has its share of such "jobbing" illustration in the contemporary mode, whatever the mode. I have surveyed all of the twentieth-century editions at the Dante Collection at the Cornell University Library (see Select List); I will mention here only those which seem to me successful in capturing some aspect of Dante's complex attitudes, and a few others that are in one way or another symbolic of different modes of unsuccess.

Beyond the range of this book is the large number of twentieth-century works that have appeared in museums and galleries with themes and imagery derived from, influenced by, or in homage to the *Inferno*. (Ludwig Volkmann speaks in his *Iconographia Dantesca* of the impossibility of a complete or comprehensive survey of such material in the nineteenth century.) A magnificent case in point is Oscar Kokoschka's *The Bride of the Wind* (Canto 5). The painting seems obviously derived from the tradition of nineteenth-century paintings of the Paolo and Francesca theme, but the title is not from Dante but from myth, and one senses deeply personal expression in this painting. One would not want to omit such paintings from an anthology of Dante illustration, and yet one cannot be sure that one has even seen all or most of such paintings. There have been, to be sure, various surveys, *Mostrae*, and *Omaggi* published in Italy from time to time on Dante illustration (see Bibliography). Giovanni Fallani has a lengthy essay on the topic, "Lectura Dantis: degli artisti contemporanei," in his *Dante Moderno* (1980). One finds, in as complete a survey as has been possible in America, some deeply interesting and truly illustrative pieces by artists of the stature of Giorgio de Chirico (Canto 1) and Pericle Fazzini (Canto 13), but, in the main, as with the Kokoschka, inspired by, not illustrative of (*illustrare*: to light up, to illuminate), the *Inferno*.

To restrict comment then to artists who have done a series of works illustrative of the *Inferno*, Ebba Holm, in a Danish edition of 1929, executed a series of woodcuts of considerable strength (in particular of the Hypocrites, Canto 23) in simplified and stylized black and white contrasts. The series of drawings done for the Modern Library Illustrated Edition of 1944 by George Grosz is somewhat disappointing from an artist of Grosz's stature. One can sense in these drawings (sometimes clearly influenced by Botticelli's) an attempt at an ironic distancing of the artist from Dante, in the sometime flippancy or whimsicality, in the sometime personal satire and symbolism; the sum: more Grosz than Dante. Much the same can be said in stronger terms about the editions by other well-known artists such as Umberto Romano (1946), Salvador Dali (1960), Richard Rauschenberg (1964), Karl Kunz (1965), Domenico Purificato (1965) and Tom Phillips (1983). The Dali and Rauschenberg, in particular, are not to be seen as illustration at all, but as complete personal recasting. More illustrative of Dante, and at the same time more pedestrian, are the colored drawings of Emma Mazza in an edition of 1956. Mazza takes the text and tone of Dante far more seriously, is perhaps more wholeheartedly involved with Dante, than is the case with many another Dantean illustrator, but the drawings often lack psychological depth. Her Capaneus, however (Canto 14), has the rage and insolence of Dante's.

Depth, seriousness, and involvement are certainly there in the *Drawings for Dante's Inferno by Rico Lebrun* (1963). John Ciardi indeed asserts in an introduction to this volume that "in Rico Lebrun the *Inferno* has finally found an essential and enduring illustrator." Such a sweeping statement can be understood only in the context of its further qualifications: "Dante's Hell is not a place but a state of being. . . . The place called Hell is another metaphor for themselves [the sinners]. . . . Hell is what they emanate by being what they are." This is a bit too twentieth-century. It allows for the admiration of Dante's sense of the tragic in human existence without Dante's faith, and renders almost unnecessary for the illustrator Dante's settings. It allows for what Lebrun and his disciples (cf. Leonard Baskin and Barry Moser) do give us: drawings of the individual anguish, torment, or inadequacy in solitary human beings. I must assert my own admiration for Lebrun's drawings, their enormous power and concentration in depicting these hopeless wrecks of humanity brutalized by their own evil or by forces beyond their control (Cantos 25, 28, 29). However, while this pitiable hopelessness is certainly there at times in Dante, it is not so unrelieved, so monochromatic, so ultimately monotonous. The tragic Dante is after all relieved by the Divine Vision in the *Commedia*, the intricate doubts ever set against at least the hope of relief. Lebrun's suffering figures, beheaded, snake-entangled, have only our profound compassion. I would qualify Ciardi's position by saying that Lebrun's tragic Dante is of the depth and quality of a Michelangelo or Delacroix, but there is more to Dante than these drawings hold. Lebrun in these drawings was, it seems to me, working up symbolic images suggested by the *Inferno* for other personal expression of his own. Some cantos are not handled at all; there are numerous other drawings of Canto 25 and of Canto 28. These seem to this observer then as a brilliant, but incomplete set to the *Inferno*, preliminary to a series for a personal and modern Lebrun Hell.

Much of what is missing in Lebrun's drawings as illustration to Dante's *Inferno* is supplied by the *Disegni Danteschi* (1969) of Renato Guttuso. Conversely, Guttuso lacks much of what Lebrun gives to us. Landscape, multitudes in action, color, verve, whimsy, and sardonic comedy are Guttuso's *forte*; missing is the sense of the tragic we have in Lebrun (Cantos 3, 18, 24, 32). Guttuso's is a sophisticated, Italianate, Mediterranean temperament of the sort I tried to sketch as part of Dante earlier. The sinners bewailing their fates from Canto 3 are operatic in their display of anguish, theatrical, somewhat farcical, or burlesque. The faces in the lower right corner know what is coming, know they deserve it, and wonder if there is not some way to strike a deal to avert it. One senses that Guttuso here and elsewhere in these drawings has his friends and enemies in the faces in his Hell, both for fun and spite, the settling of old scores (as Dante does in his Hell, as Michelangelo in his). Guttuso, worldly and witty, plays a different string to Dante's bow than Lebrun, a string perhaps more often played by artists of this century in illustrating Dante than Lebrun's: the lack-tragic, the whimsical, the suspension of judgment with respect to last things. The two, Lebrun and Guttuso, seem to me the best of the Dante illustrators of the contemporary period. Yet Dante's complex tonality encompasses both Lebrun and Guttuso, and envelopes them. That this is so is testimony to Dante's supreme status as a poet.

The Dantean sculpture of Aldo Greco, as shown in Ravenna in 1974 (Cantos 3,33), is certainly more akin to Guttuso than Lebrun, towards whimsy rather than tragedy, but, as with Guttuso, intelligent and often close to Dante in tone and detail. The recent drawings by Robert Cimbalo relate tonally more to Lebrun, but bear their own stamp of witty literalism. Aligi Sassu's wit is more allusive, both to classicism and to other twentieth-century artistic styles.

Closeness to the Dantean text in tone and detail, to his complex attitudes and his descriptions: this, in summary, must be the commonsense definition for the good Dante illustration. Does this definition leave enough room for the artist as illustrator to make a work of art of an illustration? It has happened often enough in the history of *Inferno* illustration, if not always in whole compositions at least in brilliant details, to support the definition and the critical position. Much second-rate art and second-rate illustration have been ascribed to Dante's influence. Much first-rate art has been inspired by Dante; some of it can be called illustration. The limits of the definition can give it strength, as no definition is useful that does not give limits, make demarcations.

Illustrations to Dante's Inferno

Notes to the Plates

THERE IS NO ATTEMPT IN THE NOTES BELOW TO SUMMARIZE ALL OF THE SCHOLARSHIP AND criticism on Dante iconography and illustration in general or on the individual artists in particular. They are rather notes on the plates only and are intended to aid the student who is interested in comparing the plates with Dante's text and in deciding to what degree a given plate is an illustration *to* the *Inferno* or an illustration *from* it.

The field as a whole has been magnificently covered through the nineteenth century by Ludwig Volkmann in his *Iconografia Dantesca* (1893, see the Bibliography for this and all citations below), which appeared in a limited edition English version in 1899. Contemporary with the Volkmann are the splendid and hardly less comprehensive surveys in German by F. X. Kraus ("Dante's Verhältniss zur Kunst," Book 4 of his *Dante*, 1897), and Alfred Bassermann (*Dante's Spuren in Italien*, 1897),

The bibliographies of Colomb de Batines (1845–46) and Ferrazzi (1865–77) and the *Catalogue of the Dante Collection* of the Cornell University Library (1898–1900, supplement 1920) will guide the reader to all of the illustrated editions and the scholarship in the field to their dates. The Mambelli has a special annotated bibliography "Le illustrazioni della Divina Commedia" to 1930, and the Brieger, Donati, Schubring, Mariani, and Fallani to their areas of special interest (the miniatures, early editions, the fourteenth to sixteenth centuries, nineteenth century, and twentieth century). The *Enciclopedia Dantesca* (1970–76) has bibliographies and comment on illustrations under "Commedia" and on many of the major illustrators, but the bibliographies should not be considered exhaustive. Finally, the reader should know that many of the books listed in these notes, if not most, are difficult to obtain, even through interlibrary loan.

Specific comment or bibliographic information on individual artists, periods, or styles in the Dantean context may be found in the following:

Miniatures: Auvray, Bassermann, Berenson, Brieger, M. L. D'Ancona, Donati, *Enciclopedia Dantesca*, Hughes, Koch, Kraus, Meiss, Morel, Pope-Hennessy, Salmi, Samek-Ludovici, Schubring, Singleton, Toesca, Volkmann.
Early Editions: Bassermann, Berenson, *Catalog of the Dante Collection* (Cornell),

28

Clark, Colomb de Batines, Donati, *Enciclopedia Dantesca*, Fogolari, Kraus, Lippmann, Mambelli, Pollard, Schubring, Volkmann.

Early Frescos: Bassermann, Bertolini, Koch, Kraus, Meiss, Volkmann.

Nardo di Cione: Bassermann, *Enciclopedia Dantesca*, Gronau, Koch, Kraus, Meiss, Volkmann.

F. Traini: Bassermann, Bertolini, Kraus, Meiss, Volkmann.

Botticelli: Berenson, Clark, Donati, *Enciclopedia Dantesca*, Kraus, Lippmann, Venturi, Volkmann.

Signorelli: Apollonio, Bassermann, *Enciclopedia Dantesca*, Fogolari, Kraus, Rotondi, Salmi, Schubring, Venturi, Volkmann.

Michelangelo: Bassermann, Kraus, Volkmann.

Stradanus: Biagi, *Enciclopedia Dantesca*, Kraus, Symonds, Volkmann.

Zuccaro: Bassermann, Colomb de Batines, DeSanctis, *Enciclopedia Dantesca*, Kraus, Ricci, Schubring, Volkmann.

1757 ed.: Colomb de Batines, Cornell *Catalog*, Kraus, Volkmann.

Reynolds, Fuseli, Flaxman & Blake: Toynbee.

Flaxman: Chan, *Enciclopedia Dantesca*, Kraus, Mambelli, Symmons, Toynbee, Volkmann, Yeats.

Blake: *Enciclopedia Dantesca*, Klonsky, Kraus, Roe, Toynbee, Ulivi, Volkmann, Yeats.

Ademolli: *Eniclopedia Dantesca*, Volkmann.

Delacroix: *Enciclopedia Dantesca*, Kraus, Schneider, Seznec, Volkmann.

Pinelli: *Enciclopedia Dantesca*, Kraus, Mariani, Plunkett, Volkmann.

Koch: *Enciclopedia Dantesca*, Kraus, Locella, Valle, Volkmann.

Rossetti: *Enciclopedia Dantesca*, Kraus, Locella, Volkmann.

Feuerbach: Kraus, Locella, Volkmann.

Doré: *Enciclopedia Dantesca*, Gosling, Kraus, Mambelli, Mariani, Volkmann.

Scaramuzza: *Enciclopedia Dantesca*, Ferrazzi, Kraus, Mambelli, Scartazzini, Volkmann.

Rodin: Benedite, *Enciclopedia Dantesca*.

Dargent: Volkmann.

Stassen: Elwert.

Groz: Elwert.

Dali: *Enciclopedia Dantesca*, Fallani, Gosebruch, Ulivi.

Lebrun: Baskin, Ciardi (see Lebrun), Ulivi.

Rauschenberg: *Enciclopedia Dantesca*, Fallani, Gosebruch, Ulivi.

Kunz: Ulivi.

Guttuso: *Enciclopedia Dantesca*, Fallani, Ulivi.

A. Greco: Perrone.

Sassu: Gizzi.

COMEDIA DI DANTE
ALIGIERI PRIMO CANTO
DELLA PRIMA CANTICA
DETTA INFERNO.

ALLEGORIA.

SANS, PEr lo mezzo del camino s'intende la metà della uita noſtra. Per la ſelua oſcura il uitio, nel qual l'huomo uigoroſamente preuale in quell'età. Per gl'animali, i tre uitij capitali, cioè, l'auaritia, la ſuperbia, & la luſſuria, i quali non laſciano che noi poſſiamo ſalire il monte della virtù ch'è difficile & aſpro. Per Virgilio mandato da Lucia ſi comprende la dottrina dataci da Dio, accioche col ſuo mezzo conoſciamo, & n'aſtegnamo da' uitij, & che con la ſua guida s'indirizziamo a buona uia, ſecondo che poſſono le forze noſtre.

LAND. ABBIAmo narrato non ſolamente la uita del poëta & il titolo del libro & che coſa ſia poeta, ma quanto ſia antica, nobile & uaria: quanto utile cotal dottrina, quanto efficace a mouere l'humana mente: & quanto diletti ogni liberale ingegno. Ne giudichiamo da tacere quãto in ſi diuina diſciplina ſia ſtata la eccel

ARGOMENTO.

HAuendo Dante ſmarrita la uia diritta in una oſcuriſsima ſelua, moſtra di trouar Virgilio, dal quale, raccomandatoſi a lui, fu tolto in protettione, & difendendolo dalle fiere che lo haueuano aſſalito, promette di fargli ueder l'Inferno, & il Purgatorio, & che in ultimo ſarebbe poi guidato da Beatrice nel Paradiſo.

 EL MEZZO *del camin di noſtra uita*
Mi ritrouai per una ſelua oſcura;
Che la diritta via era ſmarrita;
Et quanto a dir qual'era, è coſa dura

Eſta ſelua ſeluaggia, & aſpra, & forte;
Che nel penſier rinoua la paura.
Tant'è amara, che poco è piu morte,
Ma per trattar del ben ch'i ui trouai,
Dirò de l'altre coſe, ch'io v'hoſcorte.

camino & che coſa ſia ſelua. di che ueggio nõ piccola differétia eſſere ſtata tra gli eſpoſitori di queſta cática. Perche alcuni dicono, che il mezzo della uita humana è il ſonno, moſſi: credo dalla ſententia d'Ariſtotile nell'Etica, neſſuna differentia eſſer tra felici, & miſeri nella metà della uita: perche le notti che ſono la metà del tempo c'inducono ſonno: & da quello naſce che ne bene ne male ſentir poſſia mo. Perche uogliono che il poeta póga il mezzo della uita per la notte, & la notte pel ſonno a notare che queſto poema nõ ſia altro che una uiſione che gli apparue dormédo, per laquale hebbe cognitione delle coſe da lui ſcritte in queſte tre comedie. Dicono ad un que che imita Giouãni Euangeliſta, ilquale dormendo ſul petto di Chriſto hebbe uiſion delle coſe celeſti, oueramente ponga la notte dimoſtrando hauer cominciato il ſuo poema di notte, nella quale raccogliédoſi l'animo in ſe medeſimo & liberandoſi da ogni cura meglio intenda. Ma benche tal ſententia quadri al poeta, nondimeno le parole non la dimoſtrono ſe non con tanta ambiguità: che nõ par degna della elegantia di tanto poeta. Prima perche non

1544 ed., Venice, woodcut (from 1564 ed.).

1

Canto 1

In general these notes comprise comment on the success of the illustrator in capturing the psychological tone or attitude of the character or author through expression, gesture, landscape, or atmosphere. The premise is that it is not enough only to incorporate iconographic details from Dante's text and dispose these in aesthetically pleasing relationships. With respect to Canto I specifically, the attitudes of anxiety, terror, doubt, a wrestling with one's self or soul, are at the core of the canto, and the better illustration will convey these attitudes; the poorer will deal with peripheral detail or use Dantean motifs to make personal statements. One cannot reread lines 4–72 of Canto 14 concerning Capaneus and the other Blasphemers without realizing that the artist of the Vatican MS 4776 is trying to work with Dante's text, to give Dante's attitudes a visual embodiment, while Blake is using Dante's text as a vehicle for the expression of Blake's own contrasting attitudes towards the Capaneus symbol. Similarly, in Canto I, Blake's Virgil is not Dante's. Dante's Virgil has the limitations of human reason and is deprived of heavenly illumination. Blake's Virgil demonstrably represents poetic vision rather than reason (which Blake sees as the enemy to imagination or vision): thus the ethereal, angelic Virgil of Blake's Canto I illustration.

Botticelli's drawing for Canto 1 has, in its serial narrative technique, five representations of Dante (the second obliterated); these Dantes are closer in tone to Dante's character than Blake's. Doré's two Dantes come even closer. Botticelli's forest is beautifully drawn, but essentially decorative; Doré's forest is symbolic of the dark psychological mood of the text.

The Venetian MS illumination has great charm but no psychological penetration, the forest is not fearsome, the three beasts neither; Dante is more curious than terrified. The Lombard MS illuminations have similar charm and decorative quality, while striving also for the right psychological gestures to convey Dante's attitudes.

The 1481 printed edition copperplate engraving is clearly derived from Botticelli's drawing (using three of the Botticelli Dante figures, with the third reversed). Despite a crudeness in execution, the engraver retains much of Botticelli's grace and power, in some places even enhancing the psychological mood. The symbolic nature of Dante's dark wood of error is successfully conveyed here, and also in the Venetian 1544 edition, the Stradanus, the Crane, the de Chirico and the Cimbalo, while the 1506 edition and the Koch do not convey Dante's somber mood. The de Chirico is claustrophobic, the Manfredini, with its barren hill, alienated, the Cimbalo tangled and tortured; all doubtless speak somewhat for the individual artist, but all are dealing with moods also implicit and explicit in Dante's text. The Sienese miniature manages something like a complexity of tone in the dark background and the ubiquitous expressions on the Dante figures; the Vat. 4776 with the three beasts in a darkness is similarly effective.

Florence, Biblioteca Laurenziana, MS Plut. 40.3 (Sienese, ca. 1345).

Vatican, Biblioteca Apostolica, MS lat. 4776 (Florentine, ca. 1390–1400).

Florence, Biblioteca Riccardiana, MS 1035 (Venetian, second quarter of fifteenth century).

Paris, Bibliothèque Nationale, MS it. 2017 (Lombard, ca. 1440).

Paris, Bibliothèque Nationale, MS it. 2017 (Lombard, ca. 1440).

Sandro Botticelli, ca. 1478, Biblioteca Apostolica Vaticana.

1481 ed., Florence, copperplate engraving.

1506 ed., Florence, woodcut.

1544 ed., Venice, woodcut (from 1564 ed.).

Stradanus (Jan van der Straet), 1587, Laurentian Library, Florence.

Joseph Anton Koch, ca. 1803–25, engraving.

William Blake, 1825–27, watercolor, National Gallery of Victoria.

Gustave Doré, 1861, engraving of drawing.

41

Gustave Doré, 1861, engraving of drawing.

Walter Crane, 1892, woodcut.

Manfredo Manfredini, 1907, engraving of drawing.

G. de Chirico, 1959 ed., Rome.

Robert Cimbalo, 1984, mixed media.

2

Canto 2

The intervention of Beatrice from Heaven on Dante's behalf offers an opportunity to the illustrator for a turn to beauty and idealism and away from the ugliness, sin, pain, and tragedy dominant in the *Inferno*. Artists in tune with a transcendental romanticism, the worship of the *donna ideale,* such as Rossetti and the Pre-Raphaelites, and Anselm Feuerbach in Germany, have focused on the Beatrice figure, usually in pictorial narratives drawn from the *Vita Nuova*. I have selected here only from illustrations that have strong relationship to Dante's text. Beatrice is resplendent in the Neapolitan miniature much like Trecento depictions of the Virgin Mary; in the highly decorative Lombard initial she is depicted as an angel descending from a heaven where the Virgin, Lucia, and Rachel sit and observe. Virgil accepts Beatrice's commission in both illuminations; we have the added detail in the initial of Dante facing "Death who threatens him by the river" (ll 106–8). The evocative metaphor has caught the fancy of the Lombard artist and he gives it objective form.

We are unfortunately without Botticelli drawings for Cantos 2–7, but the 1481 engravings for these cantos, based on the Botticelli drawings, give us some idea of motifs that were in the drawings. (Botticelli's Beatrice may be seen in his drawings for the *Paradiso*). Virgil and Dante, after some hesitation on Dante's part, are about to enter Hell's gate, which has the "Through me" inscription.

Flaxman's Virgil is shrouded and muffled, suggesting a cool detachment on Flaxman's part to Dante's poem which pervades his illustrations. It is an ambiguity that can often be expected in illustrations, representing a given artist's doubts concerning Hell, sin, and punishment.

Ademolli's Beatrice is thoroughly Botticellian, projecting a great sweetness. The Koch is more mannered, Virgil consoling Dante with the support he has in heaven from the holy trio. The Batten is thoroughly imbued with the style of the Pre-Raphaelites and William Morris, and was in fact drawn during the *fin de siecle*.

1544 ed., Venice, woodcut (from 1564 ed.).

oi chui la fama ancor nel mondo dura.
e dưera quantol mondo lontana.
La mico mio e non dila uentura.
nella oiferta piaggia e impedito.
ſi nel chammin che uolto e por pagura.
E temo chel non fia gia ſi ſmarrito.
chio mi ſia tardo al ſocoorfo leuata.
por quel chio oi lui nel ciel uoito.

London, British Museum, Additional MS 19587 (Neapolitan, ca. 1370).

49

Florence, Biblioteca Nazionale, MS B.R. 39 (Lombard, ca. 1400).

1481 ed., Florence, copperplate engraving.

John Flaxman, 1793, engraving of drawing.

Joseph Anton Koch, ca. 1803–25, pen drawing.

53

Luigi Ademolli, 1817, engraving of drawing.

J. D. Batten, London, 1933 ed.

55

3

CANTO TERZO.

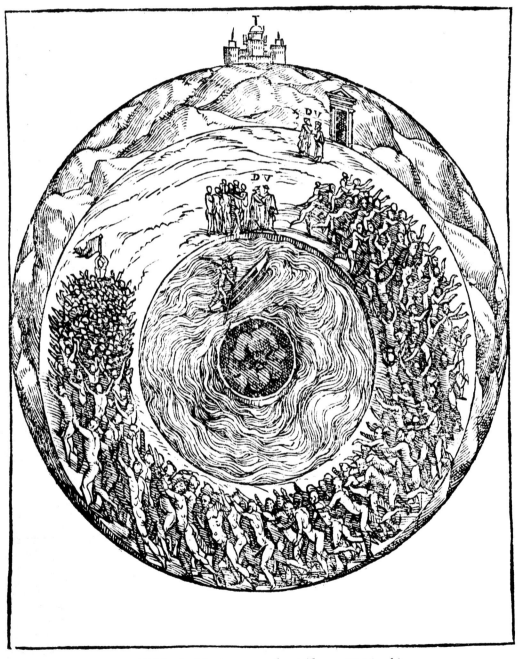

1544 ed., Venice, woodcut (from 1564 ed.).

Canto 3

Canto 3 has proven to be exceptionally rich in imagery for illustration, especially the vignettes of Dante and Virgil entering the gates of Hell, the Lukewarm chasing the wavering banner, and Charon ferrying the souls across the river Acheron. The gates to Hell have been variously depicted as a rocky entrance to a dark cave, a classical portal, or the gate of a walled medieval city. The grandiose gate of Zuccaro hints at the psychological superficiality of many of his drawings to the *Inferno*, though the Charon, heavily dependent on Michelangelo's in the *Last Judgment* (Spec. Sec.) is effective. The Vatican MS Urb. 365 miniature's gate, rather like an architectural drawing, implies the disengaged nature of the whole set of illuminations. Blake's doors are the delusive "doors of perception," the rational mind's use of sense data without vision or imagination, which is his definition of Hell. However, nothing in the drawing really conflicts with Dante's imagery and tone; this drawing of Blake's, as is often true (though not always) with Blake, is a success both for Blake's and Dante's vision.

Much the same is true for Blake's depiction of the Lukewarm: those, both human and angelic, who never took a stand for good or evil. The fainthearted angels in the sky, and the weeping, tormented humans in the foreground (including the rich and powerful) following the banner wavering in the shifting winds, whatever they mean to Blake (for which, see Roe), are sufficiently as Dante describes to be called illustrative. They are not, however, so inclusive of Dante's attitudes as the Pisan (Chantilly) miniature or in the Nardo and the Signorelli frescos (Spec. Sec.). The wind truly blows, the gnats and the worms truly bite, the angels have already turned devils in the Chantilly MS. Signorelli's devils in the Orvieto frescos are often depicted in various stages of metamorphosis from a divine or human appearance to a demonic one, not only with horns and bat wings, but in changes of flesh tones to the grey of stone, allegorizing perhaps a petrification of the heart and soul. These Lukewarm are the sinners that so moved T. S. Eliot: "I had not thought that Death had undone so many" (*Wasteland*, Canto 1, l. 63, and *Inferno*, Canto 3, l. 53). These, like all the souls of Hell, have lost the good of intellect and have abandoned hope. In their lives, they were unable to commit to anything and are now stung by the wasps of remorse and guilt.

Neither the Zuccaro nor the Scaramuzza capture this tragic tone very well. The 1481 engraving and even the 1544 woodcut, with its endless circling, capture it better. (Dante's swoon is depicted in both the 1481 and in the Zuccaro.) The Venetian miniature in the Budapest MS is well drawn, but thin as interpretation (many of the miniatures in this manuscript still have written rudimentary instructions to the illustrator, who presumably had not read the *Inferno*). The Chantilly MS and the 1481 engraving emphasize the papal crown, perhaps of Pope Celestine, who made the "grand refusal" (ll. 54–56); Aldo Greco has a wry sculpture of this hesitant Pope.

Greco's Charon captures the wild-eyed anger of Dante's old demon better than earlier renderings of him as simple devil. Michelangelo's fresco emphasizes the cruelty in Dante's Charon as he beats the sinner with his oar, a motif then copied by Zuccaro. Flaxman's drawing is influenced by the Michelangelo, and Pinelli's by both Michelangelo and Flaxman. Guttuso's Charon is faintly seen with oar lifted, and the Damned are handled with the sardonic wit mentioned in the Introduction. Sassu's Charon seems to be bringing us to a metaphysical adventure, rather than a place of suffering.

Caxi va ciel p nõ neser men bellu
nelo profondo inferno lureceue.
ebalguna gloria met aure ler telli.
Queftin nonãno fperança di morte
ela lor ciecha uita etanto baffa.
ebenudiofi fuon ognaltra forte.

Coro ax reguarda uoi una fegua.
ebeguanto conein tanto uati.
ebe ogin fua mi pailca in regni.
Epieto let uenia fi fuga nati.
dicenti ebi non ainei creduto.
ebi morte tanta nauese di fatti.
Poftia ebio nebi algun nebenofiuto.

Budapest, University Library, MS 33 (Venetian, ca. 1345).

e eni mifon morte diligere plus quā ui
tam. qui aceo uolunt mon q̄ in sume
statu mifere p̄mo condennah. Et aut
in infimo statu sint coz inuidia maise
stat q̄ inuidet oī sorti. Vn dr̄ in tertu. Ela
loz̄ cita uita e tanto bassa. chenuidioz̄ so
doqnalinsorte. Er quo q̄ isti oī sorti inui
dent. manifestum e q̄ de sua sorte ortentā
no possunt. Vn Seneca. Cui in qr̄ placet
alterius sua minimū odio sbz̄ est. Chi
nonaute ordero. chemorte tūtu nau esse di
staru. Vere nullus posset ordere quanta
est multitudo illorum qui uuulgarit̄ capt̄
ui̇ misi appellant. De quibz̄ Salomon.
Stultoz̄ isinit̄ e nūs. Tanta naḡ e mul
titudo stuloz̄ q̄ respū̄ ipoz̄ sapient̄ pauci
simi reputant. Vn tullius libro p̄mo de

d inisiam cordis qua sint talit̄ obumbra
tus q̄ inromana sede sedere nesauit.
¶ Questi scia quin̄ chemai non fur uiui.
Vere omnes homines qui dehac uita sū
fama decedunt. insti e mortui mēto ap
pellant. Vn in sin cantu xxiiij. ait auto.
Omai conuien chetuco si ti spoltr
dissel maestro ke segendo inpiuma
infama nosiuen ne sotto coltre.
Sanca laqual chisua uiten consuma
cotal uestiaio interru dise la sca
qual fammo maer e magna laschiuma.
Oms e sapientes ita se inhac uita exer
tur conantur ut p̄ glonosa facta n̄ fe
cerunt inuita post mortem inmenib;
honinū semp uiuant. Et ad hoc bn Sa
lustius incatellinario nos indūc. dicẽ.

Chantilly, Musée Condé, MS 597 (Pisan, ca. 1345).

Paris, Bibliothèque Nationale, MS it 78 (Venetian, Cristoforo Cortese, first half of fifteenth century).

*Vatican, Biblioteca Apostolica, MS Urb. lat. 365 (Gugli-
elmo Giraldi & assistants, ca. 1478).*

1481 ed., Florence, copperplate engraving.

ARGOMENTO.

SEGVENDO DANTE VIRGILIO, peruiene alla porta dello Inferno : doue dopo ha uer lette le parole spauentofe, che u'erano ſcrit te, entrano ambedue dentro. Quiui intende da Virgilio, che erano puniti gl'ignoranti : e ſe guitando il loro camino, arriuano al fiume det to Acheronte; nel quale trouò Carone, che trag getta l'anime all'altra riua. Ma come Dante ui fu giunto, ſu la ſponda del detto fiume s'addor mentò.

CANTO III.

ER me ſi ua ne la cit tà dolente :
Per me ſi ua ne l'eterno dolore :
Per me ſi ua tra la ƥer duta gente .
Giuſtitia moƒƒe'l mio Al to fattore :
Fecemi la diuina poteſtate ,
La ſomma ſapieǹtia , e'l primo amore .
D inanꜩi a me non fur coſe create ,
Senon eterne ; & io eterno duro :
Laſſate ogni ſperanꜩa uoi, che'ntrate .

I cieli e gli Angeli fu rono le co ſe inanꜩi

ALLEGORIA.
PER DANTE, CHE DIFFIDAN doſi delle ſue forꜩe, era per abandonar la Impre ƒa di ueder le coſe promeſſegli da Virgilio, ſi di moſtra, che l'huomo, ancora che egli uenuto a co gnitione della ſua ignoranꜩa, conoſca il ſuo fine eſſer lo acquiſto del ſommo bene, e deſideri di con ſeguirlo : nondimeno conſiderando le difficul ta e le fatiche, che ui entrano, da uiltà ſourapre ſo ſpeſſo rimane dall'honorato propoſto. ma nel fine confidandoſi nelle parole di Virgilio, che gli promette eſſer guida; cioè nel fauore della cele ſte gratia: prende ſicurtà di poter paſſar per lo inferno, cioè hauer conteꜩa de' uitij, da iqua li partendoſi uenga a conoſcimento della uirtù.

1555 ed., Venice, woodcut.

Federico Zuccaro, ca. 1587, Uffizi, Florence.

Federico Zuccaro, ca. 1587, Uffizi, Florence.

John Flaxman, 1793, engraving of drawing.

Bartolomeo Pinelli, 1826, engraving of drawing.

William Blake 1825–27, watercolor, Tate Gallery.

William Blake 1825–27, watercolor, National Gallery of Victoria.

Francesco Scaramuzza, 1865, pen drawing.

Emma Mazza, 1956 ed., Turin.

Renato Guttuso, 1969 ed. Rome.

Aldo Greco, 1974 ed., Ravenna.

Aldo Greco, 1974 ed., Ravenna.

Aligi Sassu, 1987 ed., Milan.

75

4

CANTO QVARTO.

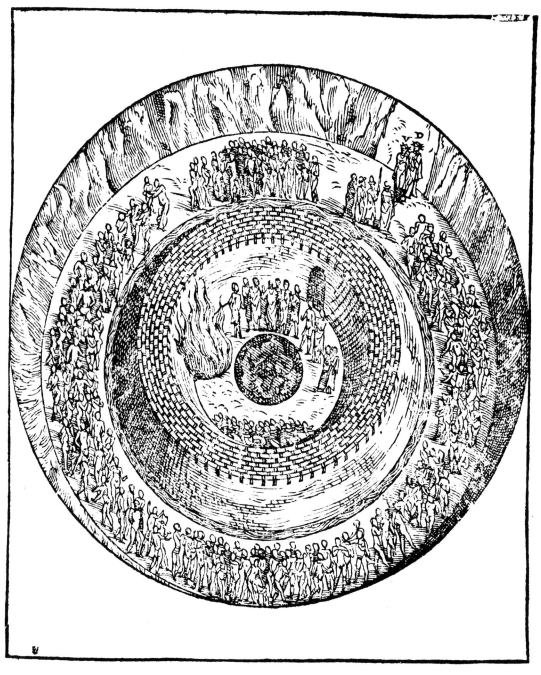

1544 ed., Venice, woodcut (from 1564 ed.)

76

Canto 4

Limbo is the eternal home of Virgil and the other great classical poets and thinkers whom Dante admires; that they and the other unbaptized are here, cut off from God, is both tragic and pitiful to Dante. A true illustration should capture these attitudes of sadness and pity, while also establishing the worth and dignity of Limbo's inhabitants. Within a seven-walled city (representing, presumably, the seven liberal arts and seven political virtues), lit dimly by the light of human reason and philosophy, Dante and Virgil interview Homer (the war poet with sword), Lucan, Ovid, and Horace in a garden landscape.

Nardo di Cione's fresco (Spec. Sec.), largely copied by Vatican 4776, conflates many of these details and, in almost ludicrously confined space, both still manage a sense of the canto's seriousness, as the separate circles of Heroes and Sages carry on discussions. Doré's garden is vaster, the atmosphere sadder, darker, perhaps more Dantesque. Stradanus's drawing is even more melancholy; within the seven concentric walls the souls of early genius seem to be inhabiting a prison yard. The Budapest MS and the Vat. 365 MS miniatures and the 1757 engraving all stress the dignity of the souls in Limbo, but the sense of tragedy is almost gone in the 1757 rendering.

Blake's poets have the sanctuary of their grove at the bottom half of the picture; above the trees are floating figures in the smoky air who represent, presumably, the Lustful of Canto 5 (but on these, see also Roe's commentary). Dante and Virgil look down from above, illustrating perhaps Dante's lines 7–12 of Canto 4 concerning a "dolorous abyss, the desolate chasm . . . So depthless-deep and nebulous and dim." This abyss is magnificently depicted in the Manfredini, who in general is at least the equal to Doré in conveying deep and dizzying space in the *Inferno*.

Budapest, University Library, MS 33 (Venetian, ca. 1345)

Vatican, Biblioteca Apostolica, MS lat. 4776 (Florentine, ca. 1390–1400)

Vatican, Biblioteca Apostolica, MS Urb. lat. 365 (Guglielmo Giraldi & assistants, ca. 1478).

1544 ed., Venice, woodcut (from 1564 ed.).

Stradanus (Jan van der Straet) 1587, Laurentian Library, Florence.

81

1757 ed., Venice, engraving.

William Blake, 1825–27, watercolor, Tate Gallery.

Gustave Doré, 1861, engraving of drawing.

Manfredo Manfredini, 1907, engraving of drawing.

5

CANTO QVINTO.

1544 ed., Venice, woodcut (from 1564 ed.).

Canto 5

The Minos of Vatican 4776 has the horns and talons and hair of a beast, in addition to the tail which Dante emphasizes. Minos in Dante's Hell judges in which circle of Hell the given sinner belongs and wraps his tail about himself that number of times. (Such a Minos bears little relation to the classical Minos, save that that Minos was a judge and had a bestial parent.) Vatican 4776 is a close rendering of Nardo's fresco, both having Minos hold an hourglass (why is not clear, since all punishment in Hell is for eternity). The Minos of the Lombard miniature is more human-appearing; Signorelli's Minos, with his bat wings, is half-and-half. The Minos of the 1544 edition, the Michelangelo fresco, and the Doré engraving are all more human than bestial in appearance; it is the Signorelli, the Michelangelo, and the Doré that capture the grim power the Minos symbol has for Dante (cf. the Cimbalo Minos, Canto 27).

The Paolo and Francesca episode has been the theme for illustrations, art, and music far more than any other Dantean motif (see Locella). One can, of course, expect much personal response to the theme of love and sexual passion overcoming moral obligation; one can expect, too, much debate as to precisely what *Dante's* attitudes are to this episode (see Santayana, pp. 108–10 and T. S. Eliot, pp. 165–66). The fact that the lovers are placed in Hell for eternity, added to the fact that Dante swoons with pity at their fate, implies both ambivalence and complexity of attitude on Dante's part. (Here, as elsewhere in the *Inferno*, there may or may not be some ironic distance between Dante the poet and Dante the wayfarer.) The Lombard miniature focuses on Dante's swoon with less theatricality than the Flaxman, the Blake, or the Pinelli. The multitudes swirling forever in the dirty wind include in the Lombard miniature the four queens mentioned by Dante (V:ll.52–64). The Vatican 4776 has an effective design based on the Nardo fresco with the multitudes of lovers reduced to a few who circle hand in hand. The Blake and the Doré are detailed, depicting various pairs of lovers in various embraces and torments, but Doré is more literal to Dante, Blake having the lovers flow upward from waters not mentioned in Dante (for these "waters of generation," see Roe).

The Ademolli, the Rossetti, and the Feuerbach have the lovers fully clothed not from any prudery on the artists' part, but, I think, in an attempt to exalt them, to distinguish them from the common sinners in Hell. Similarly clothed with some sort of Romantic Idealism are the lovers in the popular paintings of Ary Shaeffer and George Watts; the cloaking in the Kokoschka seems more a protective covering against some sort of negative force. Rodin's sculpture has both the sweet sensuality of the young body of Francesca and the gesture of shame, the averted gaze, of Paolo. Doré's Paolo is clearly the more controlled of the two lovers, while in the Manfredini he clearly is not. In the Cimbalo, the lovers, back to back, appear as much alienated as together.

Vatican, Biblioteca Apostolica, MS lat. 4776 (Florentine,
ca. 1390–1400).

Vatican, Biblioteca Apostolica, MS lat. 4776 (Florentine,
ca. 1390–1400)

Paris, Bibliothèque Nationale, MS it. 2017 (Lombard, ca. 1440).

Paris, Bibliothèque Nationale, MS it. 2017 (Lombard, ca. 1440).

*Paris, Bibliothèque Nationale, MS it. 2017 (Lombard, ca.
1440).*

1544 ed. Venice, woodcut (from 1564 ed.).

John Flaxman, 1793, engraving of drawing.

Luigi Ademolli, 1817, engraving of drawing.

Bartolomeo Pinelli, 1826, engraving of drawing.

William Blake 1825–27, watercolor, Birmingham Art Gallery.

Ary Shaeffer, 1834, Paolo and Francesca, *oil, Wallace Collection.*

Dante Gabriel Rossetti, 1849, Paolo and Francesca, *watercolor Tate Gallery.*

Gustave Dore, 1861, engraving of drawing.

Gustave Doré, 1861, engraving of drawing.

Gustave Doré, 1861, engraving of drawing.

Anselm Feuerbach, 1864, Paolo and Francesca, *oil,*
Schack-Galerie Munich.

George Frederick Watts, 1882, Paolo and Francesca, *oil, Manchester City Art Gallery.*

Auguste Rodin, 1886, Paolo and Francesca *Paris, Musée Rodin.*

Manfredo Manfredini, 1907, engraving of drawing.

Oscar Kokoschka, 1914, The Bride of the Wind, *oil, Kunstmuseum, Basel.*

Robert Cimbalo, 1984, mixed media.

6

CANTO SESTO.

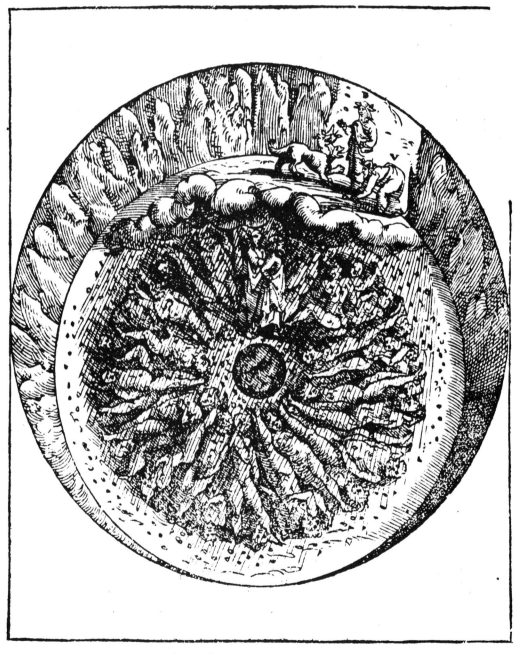

1544 ed. Venice, woodcut (from 1564 ed.).

Canto 6

The classical Cerberus was a three-headed dog that guarded the Underworld. By Dante's time, there had grown up alternate traditions of representation of Cerberus as devil with bat wings (as in Nardo's fresco) or as fanciful monster. Dante's description of Cerberus with bloodshot eyes, beard, bloated belly, and talons implies this last tradition, where in some representations Cerberus even has one or more human heads. Dante's Cerberus punishes specifically the Gluttonous (not the deepest of sins) so that among the fanciful monsters here presented, Blake's huge, ravenous beast might seem exaggerated. The Flaxman (with the serpent's tails) and the Manfredini (with the flowing beards) may be closer to Dante's conception.

One does not find often enough in the representations of the Gluttonous, and of Ciacco the Hog specifically, clear symbols of their excess, dissoluteness, and dissipation. The Venetian ms shows bloat in the prone wastrels; their flaccid lumping together is effective in the Paduan ms; likewise effective the dirty hair and the enervated expressions in the Ademolli, and the slime dripping from Ciacco in the muck in the Purificato. The dismal atmosphere of the putrid rain and stench is well caught in the Lombard and della Quercia (Yates-Thompson ms) miniatures. The Nardo fresco, usually following Dante's text so closely, has the Gluttonous at a feasting table eating and drinking, a motif also seen in F. Traini's fresco at the Camposanto in Pisa and in the Vatican 4776 miniature, and elsewhere, but not in Dante's text.

Venice, Biblioteca Marciana, MS it. IX.276 (Venetian, late fourteenth century).

Padua, Biblioteca del Seminario, MS 67 (Padua, early fif-teenth century).

Paris, Bibliothèque Nationale, MS it. 2017 (Lombard, ca. 1440).

London, British Museum, Yates Thompson MS 36 (Priamo della Quercia, mid-fifteenth century).

John Flaxman, 1793, engraving of drawing.

Luigi Ademolli, 1817, engraving of drawing.

William Blake, 1825–27, watercolor, Tate Gallery.

Manfredo Manfredini, 1907, engraving of drawing.

Domenico Purificato, 1964 ed., Rome.

M. Michael 1975 ed. Ravenna.

7

CANTO SETTIMO.

1544 ed., Venice, woodcut (from 1564 ed.).

117

Canto 7

Plutus, the classical god of wealth, is depicted by Dante as inflated, enraged, and spouting demonic gibberish till collapsing instantly at Virgil's rebuke. Various illuminations portray Plutus as traditional devil. The Chantilly MS rendering is a brilliant *jeu d'esprit:* Plutus is inflated, gross, and sits upon a throne of moneybags with ecclesiastic crozier and miter. Dante's emphasis on the hoarding and wasting in the Church is thus highlighted by the Lombard artist, as it is by Nardo and Vatican 4776 with the depictions of miters, capes, and tonsures. Doré's substituting of moneybags for the huge rocks, which the hoarders and wasters push at one another, is clearly a lark, in the tradition of the Lombard miniaturist. The animated rendering in the Chantilly MS of the absurd, Sysiphus-like struggle between the Hoarders and Wasters takes on particular poignancy because of the sinners who are caught in the middle.

The Vatican 4776 is certainly derived from the Nardo Fresco, both having the tonality of sardonic comedy. The pen drawing is considered by Professor Meiss to be by a different hand than the finished miniature, but, if so, the two are well within both Nardo's and Dante's ambience.

The Brescia woodcut of 1487, perhaps influenced by the 1481 edition's engravings (though much cruder), is meant to be read counter-clockwise beginning at top right, Plutus as devil is defeated, Dante and Virgil stroll past the weeping clerics and others at their task with the stones, while Phlegyas the boatman waits to take Dante and Virgil across the river Styx. I have included the plate to serve as representative of the body of woodcut editions of the late-fifteenth through the sixteenth centuries, none of which ever rise to the level of true illustration.

The antagonists in the 1544 are at rest, though poised and ready for conflict; Plutus seems thoroughly human. The Stradanus has the two figures in the foreground taunting one another, as Dante has one who wastes asking his antagonist, "Why do you hoard?" while the Hoarder asks "Why do you waste?" In the Scaramuzza the questioner at the right accompanies his question with appropriate Italian gesture, while the others exhibit various sorts of stubbornness. The Holm does not have the one-on-one collisions of the text, but more of an endless treadmill parade. The Cimbalo renders a physicality to the scene through the antagonists' overdeveloped neck and back muscles.

Chantilly, Musée Conde, MS 597 (Pisan, ca. 1345).

Chantilly, Musée Conde, MS 597 (Pisan, ca. 1345).

Vatican, Biblioteca Apostolica, MS lat. 4776 (Florentine, ca. 1390–1400).

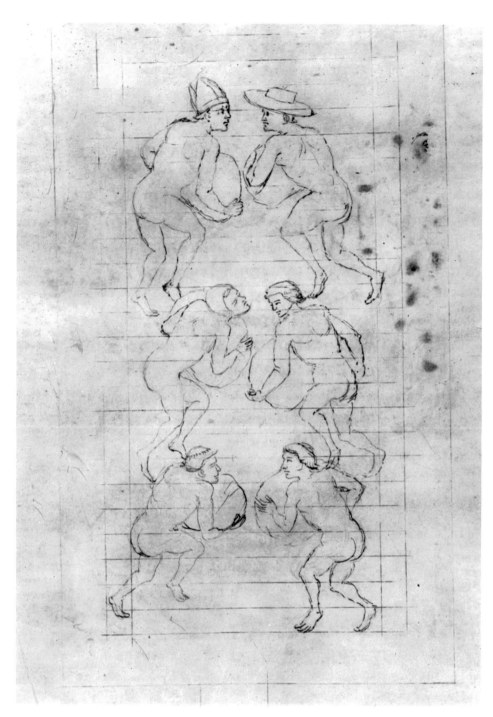

Vatican, Biblioteca Apostolica, MS lat. 4776 (Florentine, ca. 1390–1400).

1487 ed., Brescia, woodcut.

121

Stradanus (Jan van der Straet) 1587, Laurentian Library,
Florence.

Federico Zuccaro, ca. 1587, Uffizi, Florence.

Gustave Doré, 1861, engraving of drawing.

Francesco Scaramuzza, 1865, pen drawing.

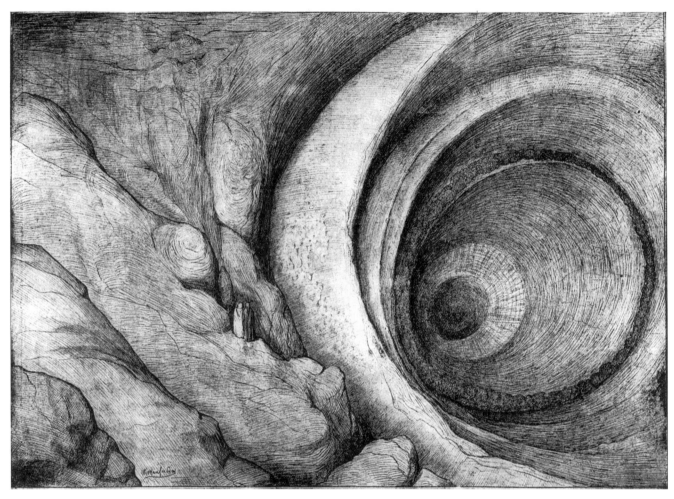

Manfredo Manfredini, 1907, engraving of drawing.

Ebba Holm, 1929, woodcut.

Robert Cimbalo, 1984, mixed media.

Notes to the Special Section

I refer the reader to the brief general remarks in my Introduction on the tradition of the "Hell" or "Last Judgment" frescos or panels (pp. 17–18). Volkmann and Kraus handle the tradition with comprehensiveness; the Brieger updates the scholarship on the tradition. My notes to the specific cantos contain commentary on some of the illustrations in this section.

In the pre-Dante Baptistery mosaic, we find sinners roasted on spits, cut in half by devils with saws, or hung by their heels. None of these motifs is in Dante. There is a devil blowing a horn at the upper right, a motif given to the Earth Giant in Dante.

Giotto, in the Paduan fresco done just before the writing of the *Inferno*, has sinners hanging by the tongue, hair, or penis, devils drilling through, or pouring molten gold into, the mouth: details not in Dante's text, but often repeated in "Last Judgments" or "Infernos" before and after Dante. In the lower right-hand corner we do, however, find details at least reminiscent of Dante's *Inferno*, Cantos 21–22, the Grafters, and 24–25, the Thieves. Volkmann notes that Giotto's stream of fire which flows from the left hand of God is directly traceable to older Byzantine prototypes.

The sinners punished in the four conical pits at the bottom border of the Giotto fresco probably influenced the design of the Traini fresco later at the Camposanto in Pisa (Giotto's influence can be seen elsewhere in comparing the two frescos). In general, repeated motifs in all of the "Hell" or "Last Judgments" here represented suggested a painter's tradition which was more influential than Dante's text. The subject needs a close comparative study, though this is not the place for it (see my article in *Dante Studies*, CXI, 1993).

I can add little to Volkmann's comments on the very influential Camposanto fresco of Francesco Traini:

> The whole is divided by stone piers into sections, but this arrangement had been usual before Dante's time. Satan certainly is here a hairy monster which swallows sinners with its triple jaws. Among the doomed, too, we find some who mutually lacerate each other or are fettered with snakes; and besides these, there are many other features which also appear in Dante. For example, there is among the sinners one who holds his head "in guisa di lanterna" in his hand, and another whose body is ripped so that the entrails hang out; in these critics have seen Bertram de Born and Mahomet, and have considered that the connection with the "Divine Comedy" was as good as proved. If closer attention had been given to the matter, there would have been discovered on the ribbon—which the alleged Bertram de Born waves like a standard—the inscription, "Ariano heretico ogni altro," and close to the so-called Mahomet the annotation, "Simoniaci." Mahomet, on the contrary, lies here bound on the ground, specified by his turban and the annotation "Maometto," while Dante represents him in the above mutilated condition. The punishment of the seers is also different from that in the "Comedy": there we see them with their faces turned upwards; here we find, as the betokening sign of their mental infatuation, that their eyes are surrounded with snakes. There are also in the picture numerous punishments which find no place in Dante, and are taken rather from the traditional, hideously fantastic Hell; for example, there is a man roasting on the spit, another who is being sawn asunder, a miser into whose mouth liquid metal is being poured, chained gluttons seated before a well-garnished table, and many more.

These latter motifs we have seen in the Baptistery mosaic and in the Giotto fresco. These then and many others in the Camposanto fresco are used in "Inferno" frescos by Giovanni da Modena in Bologna, by Taddeo di Bartolo in San Gimignano, and in panels by Fra Angelico in Florence and Giovanni di Paolo in Siena.

In all of these cases, hints for punishments are taken from Dante and used for the artist's own purposes as he works within the "Hell" or "Last Judgment" tradition, adding his own originality in composition and detail. Traini's running kings in the lower right corner certainly owe something to Dante's Lukewarm of Canto 3, his men without heads something to Dante's Sowers of Discord, his men in a pit to Dante's Grafters. How much to Dante, and how much to Giotto or another artist, how much to the artist's own originality, is the question.

Volkmann's comments on the Bologna and San Gimignano frescos are then to be understood not as denying Dante's influence, but debunking the earlier scholarly position that Dante's influence is dominant:

> The large representation of Hell in the Cappella Bolognini in S. Petronio at Bologna, which dates from the commencement of the fifteenth century, shows a close resemblance to the fresco at Pisa. . . . Here also we notice countless seeming imitations of Dante, which, however, vanish on nearer examination. A sinner who holds his head in his hand, as with Bertram de Born in Dante, is called Dathan; near him we can see Abiron, who entered with him into a conspiracy against Moses and Aaron. Men whose bodies are ripped open are meant to represent the desecrators of the temple, as the word *sacralecy* shows, not the instigators of discord, as with the poet. Mahomet, on the other hand, lies, worried by serpents, on the ground. On the right, at the top, a devil is carrying by the legs one of the damned, whom he has pitched on to his back head downwards. Involuntarily one's thoughts revert to the Elder of Lucca in the twenty-first canto of the Inferno, whom a devil throws, in like manner, into the seething pitch; but the note names him Simon Magus, while, in the "Comedy," the Simonists stand in circular holes, their feet licked painfully by the flames. Satan himself is not the Satan of Dante: he has only one face, has no wings, and is bound with chains to the rocks. Lastly, there are a number of torments of the most varied description which Dante does not mention. . . . the great fresco of San Gimignano, divided into three parts, is likewise very different from Dante's Hell, and represents, among other things, a sinner being sawn asunder, a covered table surrounded by famishing people, the yawning jaws of Hell which gobble up the sinners, and many other traditional torments, sometimes thought out with the most nauseous delight.

"Nauseous" is debatable; "with vulgarity and verve" is perhaps better. Certainly Dante would have approved in the Bartolo the punishment of the avaricious man by strangulation with the cord of his moneybag, or the gluttonous, obese man having food forced down his throat. The devil whipping the adulterous woman is quite in line with Dante's text.

Fra Angelico's *Last Judgement* panel in San Marco, Florence, is organized almost completely after Traini's fresco, as a close comparison will show, the Angelico a simplification of the Traini. The beehive layout of the Angelico Hell is perhaps a consequence of the simplification. Angelico's Satan is, however, immersed in a well-like structure more like the Nardo fresco and Dante's text than Traini's full-length beast. Snakes entwine the sinners throughout, and, as with the Traini, some of the details are doubtless borrowed from Dante for the artist's own free use.

Giovanni di Paolo's panel in Siena is clearly indebted to the Angelico (perhaps, too, to the Nardo fresco) exhibiting the usual conglomeration of sources and personal genius:

> [There are] . . . motives which can perhaps be explained only by an acquaintance with Dante's poem: reclining souls, on which descend flakes of fire; souls engaged in biting themselves, and a group of two sinners, one of whom bites the other's head as Ugolino bites Roger; souls swimming in water, others scourged by a demon or riven by the claws of a monster; at the entrance to Hell a devil with wings and a tail, with which he—a frequent misunderstanding—embraces a sinner, while before him are two souls—evidently Minos;

lastly, sinners rolling heavy stones. At the same time there are considerable deviations: the usual spread table, a soul ridden by a devil, and particularly, in the lower right-hand corner, a man who is pecked in the ribs by an eagle, like Prometheus. A wonderful conglomeration of the old Hell of tradition, of the Inferno of Dante, and the Hades of the ancients! (Volkmann, p. 19)

John Pope-Hennessy in his *Giovanni di Paolo* (1938) attempts to read all of the detail of the panel as purposely illustrative of Dante's specific cantos. The readings are quite loose and unconvincing, but Pope-Hennessy's summary statement seems quite apt for Paolo, Angelico, Nardo, and the others: "All the scenes are realized with extraordinary vigor, and the variety of the postures of the naked bodies are . . . little short of astonishing".

The Nardo di Cione (Bernardo Orcagna) fresco is a careful and extraordinary attempt to illustrate all of the *Inferno,* as I have tried to make clear in my Introduction and throughout the canto notes. I add here only that the vignettes from the cantos unfold in a descending order and that Dante and Virgil are not present in Nardo's full depiction of the circles of Hell.

The frontispiece to the Fruosino MS is in all particulars modeled after the Nardo fresco, save that Dante and Virgil appear five times in the Fruosino. Note that the table of the Gluttons appears in both the Nardo and the Fruosino, as it does in the Traini and Angelico, though not in Dante. It is testimony to the power of the painterly tradition that the artist, Nardo, most faithful to Dante's text makes use of this traditional, non-Dantean motif.

The Signorelli and Michelangelo details have been discussed in the Introduction and the notes to Canto 3.

Florence, Baptistery, mosaic, 13th century.

*Giotto and assistants, fresco, Last Judgement, Hell detail.
Scrovegni Chapel, Padua, ca. first decade of 14th century.*

*Francesco Traini, fresco, Hell. Camposanto, Pisa, ca.
1340s.*

Nardo di Cione, fresco, Hell. Florence, S. Maria Novella,
Strozzi Chapel, ca. 1350s.

Nardo di Cione, fresco, Hell. Florence, S. Maria Novella,
Strozzi Chapel, ca. 1350s.

*Nardo di Cione, fresco, Hell. Florence, S. Maria Novella,
Strozzi Chapel, ca. 1350s.*

*Vatican, Biblioteca Apostolica, MS lat. 4776. Florentine,
ca. 1390–1400.*

Paris, Bibliothèque Nationale, MS.it. 74. Florentine, Bartolomeo di Fruosino, ca. 1420.

Paris, Bibliothèque Nationale, MS.it. 74. Florentine, Bartolomeo di Fruosino, ca. 1420.

Fra Angelico, wall panel, Hell. Florence, San Marco, 1430s.

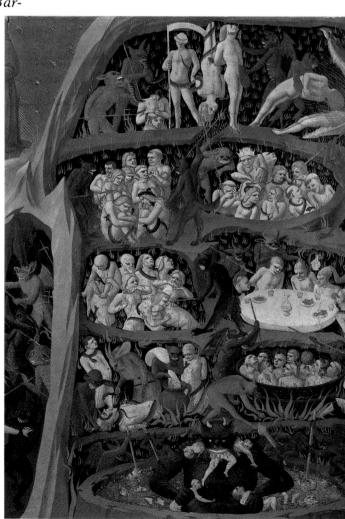

Giovanni di Paolo, wall panel, Hell. Siena, Pinacoteca, 1453.

Luca Signorelli, fresco. Orvieto, Duomo, first decade of 16th century.

Luca Signorelli, fresco. Orvieto, Duomo, first deca 16th century.

Eugene Delacroix, oil, Dante's Bark. *Paris, Louvre, 1822.*

chelangelo, fresco, Last Judgement detail. Vatican, Sis-
e Chapel, 1540s.

*Francesco Traini, fresco, Hell. Camposanto, Pisa, ca.
1340s.*

...ovanni da Modena, fresco, Hell. Bologna, San Petronio,
1410.

...ancesco Traini, fresco, Hell. Camposanto, Pisa, ca.
...40s.

Taddeo de Bartolo, fresco, Hell. San Gimignano, Collegiata, 1393.

8

CANTO OTTAVO.

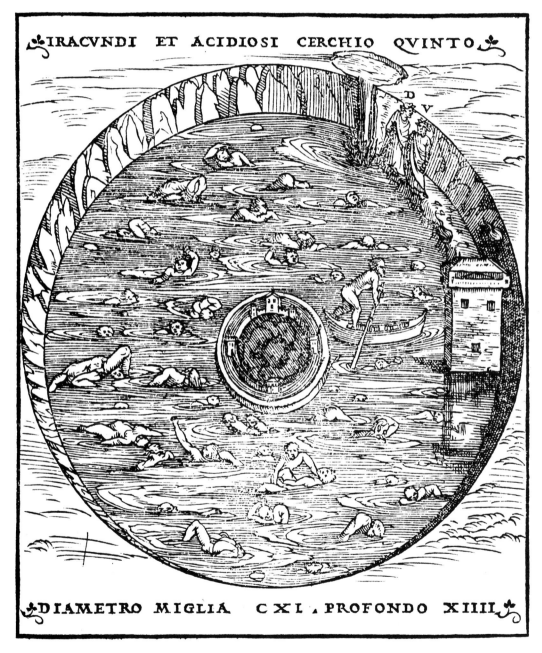

1544 ed., Venice, woodcut (from 1564 ed.).

Canto 8

Canto 8 focuses on the sin of violent anger or wrath in various aspects. Phlegyas, classically the son of Mars who in anger burned Apollo's temple, howls with rage on seeing Dante; Dante is enraged in his encounter with the wrathful Filippo Argenti because of a personal enmity with the Argenti family; the devils at the gates of the City of Dis are violently angry at the presumption of the living Dante's wanting to enter their infernal city.

The Stradanus illustrates all this anger, the rage of the sinners in the river-swamp of Styx, of the face of Phlegyas, and of Dante as he berates Argenti in the water. The 1757 edition rendering is less dark and terrifying, though the Dante-Argenti encounter is effective.

One wonders if the man on the shore in the Fruosino miniature is supposed to be Argenti, though, if so, both situation and expression seem wrong. One wonders, too, why Blake's Phlegyas is somber rather than angry, sitting rather than rowing (the answers, one expects, have little to do with Dante's text).

Delacroix's painting (Spec. Sec., discussed in the Introduction) exhibits the terrible anger of Argenti biting the boat, and of another of the Wrathful tearing at the neck of one other. Dante's expression is of both anger and shock. The magnificently painted man and woman in the water, however, only suffer. The smoky hellfire of Dis both blackens and illuminates the scene. Doré's engraving is, in places, clearly inspired by the Delacroix.

The Yates-Thompson (della Quercia) miniature has a subtle interplay between Dante and Virgil in Phlegyas's boat, where Dante's hatred for Argenti is encouraged by Virgil. (Phlegyas is almost comically hideous here.) The Cortese initial is too small and full of vignettes for subtle psychology, but there is great charm in the two vignettes on either side of the "I," particularly in the Virgil pushing Argenti away.

The sequence of frames from the 1544 edition clearly shows the ingenious methodology of refocusing, as the City of Dis's circle gets larger and larger. Psychological subtlety in individuals is absent, but a sense of endlessly unfolding and fascinating adventure is there. It is there, too, in the Flaxman, in the exhilarating sailing into the smoky, vague architecture of the City of Dis.

The Botticelli drawings reappear with Canto 8, Dante and Virgil slipping down the steep escarpment in the upper right-hand corner and entering Phlegyas's boat on the canal-like Styx amidst the wailing sinners. Virgil, then, in the lower left-hand corner, is seen first arguing with the devils and then disconsolate in being rebuffed (though the sequencing or time flow is backwards from the usual here). The graveyard of the Heretics at the lower right corner anticipates Canto 9.

130

O dico seguitante castai prima
chenoi fustimo alpie dellalta torre .
lioechi nostri nariar suso alla oma
P erdue fiammette cheuedemmo pou
eunaltra dalunci render cenno
tanto cappena ispotea lecchio torre

E t io muolsi alma ditutel senno
dissi questo che dice et che risponde
quellaltro foco echi son quei chesenno
E t elli ame superle suade onde
gia scorger puoi quello che saspetta
sel fummo deiparian nosti naschonde

Paris, Bibliothèque Nationale, MS. it. 74 (Florentine, Bartolomeo di Fruosino, ca. 1420).

131

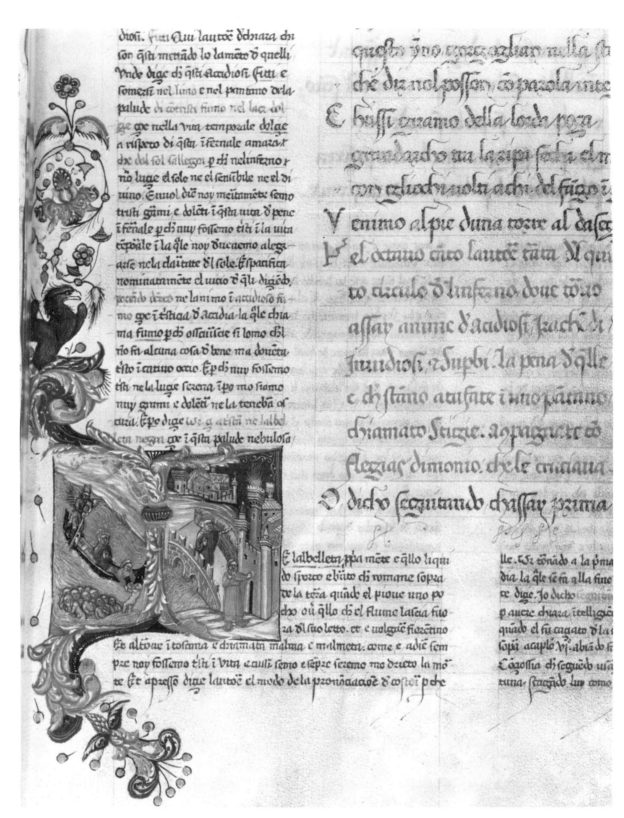

Paris, Bibliothèque Nationale, MS it 78 (Venetian, Cristoforo Cortese, ist half of fifteenth century).

132

London, British Museum, Yates Thompson MS 36 (Priamo della Quercia, mid fifteenth century).

Florence, Biblioteca Laurenziana, MS Plut. 40.1 (North Italian, 1456).

133

Sandro Botticelli, ca. 1478, Kupferstichkabinett, Staatliche Museen, Preussischer Kulturbesitz, Berlin.

134

1544 ed., Venice, woodcut (from 1564 ed.).

1544 ed., Venice, woodcut (from 1564 ed.).

136

Stradanus (Jan van der Straet), 1587, Laurentian Library, Florence.

137

1757 ed., Venice, engraving.

138

John Flaxman, 1793, engraving of drawing.

William Blake, 1825–27, watercolor, Fogg Gallery

Gustave Doré, 1861, engraving of drawing.

9

CANTO NONO.

1544 ed., Venice, woodcut (from 1564 ed.).

Canto 9

Dante's allegory of the three Furies (who have sacred functions in early Greek religious life) has been variously interpreted by Dantean commentators, and this variety is exhibited even in the two miniatures here selected. The Morgan Library MS depicts the Furies as fearsome, the Vatican 4776 as despairing. The Furies in Dante's text call upon the Gorgon's head to turn Dante's soul to stone, but the head does not appear in either of the miniatures, though Virgil covering the face of Dante from the sight of the Gorgon Medusa is rendered in the Morgan. The gate, the walls of Dis, and the guardian devils are well delineated in the Morgan MS; the angel in the Vat. 4776 MS is remarkably drawn (the Furies, though not the angel, are based on the Nardo fresco).

The two renderings of the angel in the Botticelli are even more remarkable, as is the detailing of the whole drawing. Botticelli's Furies, taken together with the devil who holds the head of the Medusa, seem to suggest sexual overtones in his interpretation of the allegory. The Wrathful battle in the waters of Styx or flee from the angel, who walks on the water. Dante and Virgil are represented in no less than six tableaux in this drawing, the last two of which are beyond the gates of Dis into the burning, walled cemetery of the Heretics. The whole is wonderfully animated. The 1481 engraving certainly borrows details from the Botticelli, but the composition is simplified and rearranged; the whole is certainly much cruder than the Botticelli. The devil bringing the Gorgon's head is at the right foreground.

The Zuccaro, with its emphasis on the fantastic gate and skeleton-like devils, conveys a serio-comic tone, as if parts of the *Inferno* are somewhat embarrassing for the artist. The Scaramuzza likewise has a touch of the comic, but for different reasons: the stylistic realism has the devils at the gate looking like street thugs in costume.

New York, the Pierpont Morgan Library, MS 676 (Italian, late fourteenth century).

Vatican, Biblioteca Apostolica, MS lat. 4776 (Florentine, ca. 1390–1400).

Vatican, Biblioteca Apostolica, MS Urb. lat. 365 (Guglielmo Giraldi & assistants, ca. 1478).

Sandro Botticelli, ca. 1478, Biblioteca Apostolica Vaticana.

1481 ed., Florence, copperplate engraving.

Federico Zuccaro, ca. 1587, Uffizi, Florence.

Francesco Scaramuzza, 1865, pen drawing.

10

CANTO DECIMO

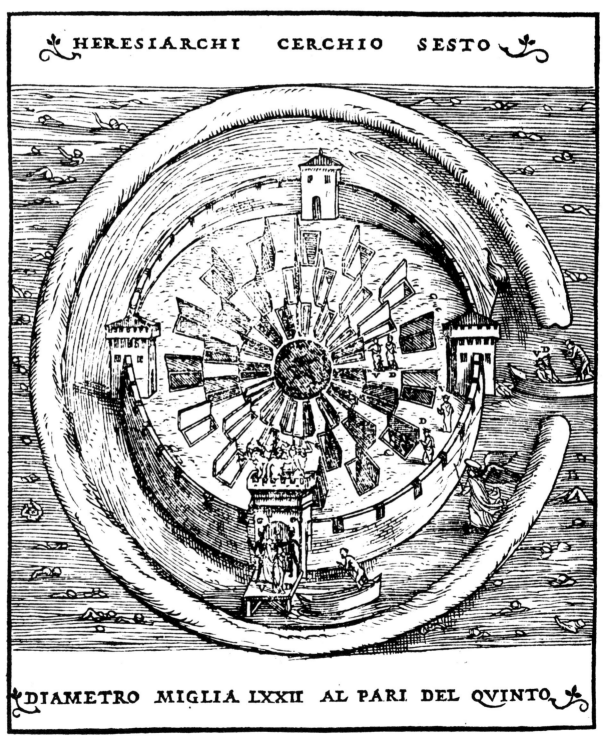

HERESIARCHI CERCHIO SESTO

DIAMETRO MIGLIA LXXII AL PARI DEL QVINTO

1544 ed., Venice, woodcut (from 1564 ed.).

Canto 10

The conversation of Dante with Farinata degli Uberti is certainly one of the greatest episodes in the *Inferno*, and its subtlety is examined in Erich Auerbach's chapter on Canto 10 in *Mimesis*. One looks in the illustrations to this episode at least for Dante's respect for Farinata, for Farinata's dignity and his "grand despite" for Hell, and for Cavalcanti's deep concern for news of his son. One does not find any really comprehensive successes.

The Vat. 4776 has a Farinata with some dignity and scorn, and a Dante with some air of respect; Virgil is properly standing aside, Cavalcanti is improperly in a burning vault of his own. There is, however, more often unintentional comedy in the confinement of the two in the same narrow vault (looking often like children playing in boxes) in the miniatures. The Fruosino has the headdresses of a cleric and a king just visible; the Vat. 365, while beautifully painted in the style of Piero della Francesca, conveys little of either pain or dignity in the depiction of the two Heretics. The Botticelli does not escape the ludicrous in the various Heretics shouting from beneath the vault covers, though they are at least suffering, and Farinata does have some measure of dignity. (The Virgil and Dante figures are colored, showing that Botticelli at first intended to make these drawings into small paintings.) Dante and Virgil are overcome by the stench from the lower Hell, and they take cover behind the tomb of Pope Anastasius.

Blake's Farinata bears some relation to Dante's, but not much, partly, no doubt, because heresy against Dante's God is to Blake a sign of imaginative wisdom. There is more of the suffering sage in Blake's Farinata than the proud and contemptuous warrior. The Doré is more successful as illustration (much praised by Gautier), though one wonders at Doré's Dante, who seems more standoffish than respectful, while Farinata seems more suffering than disdainful. The Dargent is rather crudely theatrical, though Farinata is more aggressive than in the Doré (perhaps excessively so for Dante's description).

Vatican, Biblioteca Apostolica, MS lat. 4776 (Florentine, ca. 1390–1400).

Paris, Bibliothèque Nationale, MS. it. 74 (Florentine, Bartolomeo di Fruosino, ca. 1420).

150

Vatican, Biblioteca Apostolica, MS Urb. lat. 365 (Gugliel-mo Giraldi & assistants, ca. 1478).

Sandro Botticelli, ca. 1478, Biblioteca Apostolica Vaticana.

William Blake, 1825–27, watercolor, British Museum.

Gustave Doré, 1861, engraving of drawing.

154

Yan Dargent, 1879, engraving of drawing.

155

11

CANTO VNDECIMO.

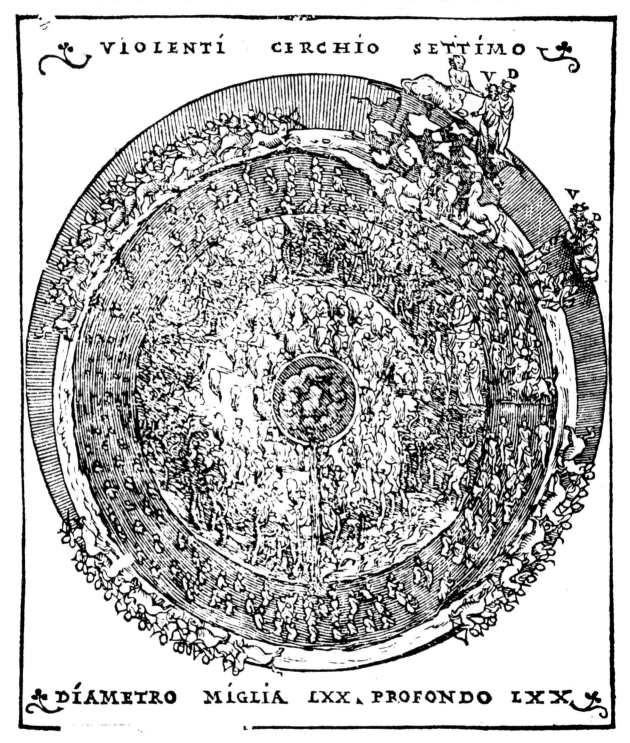

1544 ed., Venice, woodcut (from 1564 ed.).

Canto 11

The long discussion in Canto 11 between Dante and Virgil concerning the divisions of the upper and lower Hell limits the range of illustration for the canto. There has been focus on the tomb of Pope Anastasius, on the stench from, and the awesome descent to, the lower Hell, and various attempts to diagram the divisions of that lower Hell.

Botticelli's great vertical section of the cone of the whole of the *Inferno* is perhaps the inspiration for the horizontal sections of the 1544 edition and subsequent diagrams. Each division in the Botticelli has tiny figures undergoing the tortures Dante has devised for that circle or *bolgia*. The Yates-Thompson MS miniature attempts a diagram of the next three circles to come (those of the violent against others, against self, and against God). But there is no attempt to differentiate Dante's punishments for the different sorts of violence; all the sinners are transfixed on rocks.

The most successful of Canto 11 illustrations are those depicting the perilousness of the descent into the lower Hell, the narrow path downward in the Vat. 4776, the sheer cliff in the Lombard miniature, the great cleft and canyon in the Dargent, and the vast rocky precipice in the Manfredini.

Vatican, Biblioteca Apostolica, MS lat. 4776 (Florentine, ca. 1390–1400).

Imola, Biblioteca Comunale, MS 32 (Lombard ca. 1440).

London, British Museum, Yates Thompson MS 36 (Priamo della Quercia, mid-fifteenth century).

Sandro Botticelli, ca. 1478, Kupferstichkabinett, Staatliche Museen, Preussischer Kulturbesitz, Berlin.

159

Yan Dargent, 1879, engraving of drawing, detail.

Manfredo Manfredini, 1907, engraving of drawing.

12

CANTO DVODECIMO.

1544 ed., Venice, woodcut (from 1564 ed.).

Canto 12

Beneath the rocky precipice caused by an earthquake at the harrowing of Hell by Christ, lies the river of boiling blood in which are punished the Violent against others. Each is submerged to a depth proportionate to his sin. This seventh circle is guarded first by the raging Minotaur, classically with human body and head of a bull. The Lombard miniature has this reversed as do most miniatures and as do the Botticelli and the 1544 edition. The Minotaur bites his hand in rage in the Lombard, Vat. 4776 and the Botticelli, and further on in the Botticelli he charges off in anger on the rocky slope. Thereafter the sinners are watched over by Centaurs, half-man, half-horse, creatures brilliantly animated in the Botticelli. The Vat. 4776 has a dynamic composition with the three Centaurs and the Minotaur surrounding a bloody pool. Some details are clearly taken from the Nardo fresco (Spec. Sec.); one of the Centaurs bears a spear, helmet, and shield, details not mentioned by Dante, but ironically apt since many of the sinners here, such as Alexander and Attila, are punished for martial brutalities.

The Lombard miniature deftly shows the sinners in various levels of immersion, which the Vat. 365 miniature does not do, while the Botticelli and the 1544 do. The Vat. 365 has an air of tranquillity, of things under control, which does not suit the tempestuousness of the sinners and their sin. Botticelli captures this necessary turmoil much better. (The sticks of the Wood of the Suicides of Canto 13 are seen in the lower borders of the Botticelli and the 1544). The Violent in the Doré are then perhaps too passive (not so the threatening Centaurs); they are rather reminiscent of some of the sinners in the Delacroix (Spec. Sec.).

Vatican, Biblioteca Apostolica, MS lat. 4776 (Florentine, ca. 1390–1400).

Paris, Bibliothèque Nationale, MS it. 2017 (Lombard, ca. 1440).

Paris, Bibliothèque Nationale, MS it. 2017 (Lombard, ca. 1440).

Vatican, Biblioteca Apostolica, MS Urb. lat. 365 (Gugliel-mo Giraldi & assistants, ca. 1478).

Sandro Botticelli, ca. 1478, Biblioteca Apostolica Vaticana.

Gustave Doré, 1861, engraving of drawing.

13

CANTO DECIMOTERZO.

1544 ed., Venice, woodcut (from 1564 ed.).

169

Canto 13

Illustrations to Canto 13 constitute an exceptionally rich set, in part presumably because Dante's compassion and ours is especially roused by the damnation of the Suicides in general and Pier delle Vigne in particular. If one is to illustrate Dante literally, there is no Pier delle Vigne to depict, who is only a voice from a broken branch in the Wood of the Suicides. In this case, the gesture and expression of the Dante figure is crucial. Many illustrators, however, do find ways to give Pier delle Vigne and the other Suicides a human head of expression.

The Doré plates are the best examples of this latter form of poetic license which has understandably disturbed some critics, such as Volkmann. They seem to me, however, successful in conveying the enormous melancholia in the suicidal impulse and in Dante as sympathetic observer. The Manfredini, as usual influenced by the Doré, has a human head discernable in the trees, though not so mannered and exaggerated as the Doré, a bit less melancholy and perhaps a bit less effective thereby. Blake's Suicides are similarly outlined in his thorny trees, but the Pier delle Vigne looks much like Blake's Urizen head, while the other three trees embody feminine symbols, Blake, as usual, adding some personal commentary to Dante's. Ademolli's Dante suits the tenor of the Canto as does, surprisingly, that of the Vat. 365 miniature.

The Nardo fresco's Canto 13 detail has been praised in the Introduction, though it, as usual, does without a Dante figure. Dante bowing in the Vat. 4776 is effective; the head of Pier delle Vigne protruding from the tree trunk (probably borrowed from the Nardo fresco) is not. The Fruosino seems dependent on both the Nardo and the Vat. 4776. The Lombard miniature is masterful in its depiction of the Wasters of One's Goods tormented by the hounds, as are the Botticelli and the Fazzini; all three are rather intricate in design, the Botticelli perhaps to a fault. The 1544 woodcut seems influenced by the Botticelli (note the centaur at the edge of each), with Botticelli's rectangle being twisted to a circular mode.

Koch's Harpies are not so successful as others here represented, and his Pier delle Vigne is a bit stagy, though the whole is well drawn according to formulae of the Italian masters Koch imitates.

Vatican, Biblioteca Apostolica, MS lat. 4776 (Florentine, ca. 1390–1400).

Paris, Bibliothèque Nationale, MS. it. 74 (Florentine, Bartolomeo di Fruosino, ca. 1420).

Paris, *Bibliothèque Nationale, MS it. 2017 (Lombard, ca. 1440).*

172

Vatican, Biblioteca Apostolica, MS Urb. lat. 365 (Gugliel-mo Giraldi & assistants, ca. 1478).

Sandro Botticelli, ca. 1478, Biblioteca Apostolica Vaticana.

Joseph Anton Koch, ca. 1803–25, pen drawing.

Luigi Ademolli, 1817, engraving of drawing.

176

William Blake 1825–27, watercolor, Tate Gallery.

William Blake 1825–27, watercolor, National Gallery of
Victoria.

Gustave Doré, 1861, engraving of drawing.

179

Gustave Doré, 1861, engraving of drawing.

Gustave Doré, 1861, engraving of drawing.

Manfredo Manfredini, 1907, engraving of drawing.

Pericle Fazzini, 1959 ed., Rome.

14
CANTO DECIMOQVARTO.

1544 ed., Venice, woodcut (from 1564 ed.).

184

Canto 14

Most of the illustrators of Canto 14 depict the three sorts of sinners described on the arid plain under the rain of fire: the Blasphemers supine, the Usurers crouching, and the Sodomites ever walking. One of the Blasphemers, Capaneus, King of Thebes, who scorned God, continues his scornful attitude in hell. The Capaneus of Vat. 4776 has already been compared to Blake's Capaneus in the introduction and the notes to Canto One. It is only the crowned Capaneus in Vatican 4776 that shows disdain; the other sinners are disposed around him in various postures of pain. Nardo's Capaneus (Spec. Sec.) is prone with arm outstretched, as the others strive to avoid the rain of fire. Capaneus seems absent from Fruosino's miniature; the Wood of the Suicides is in the background, and a branch of Phlegethon, the river of boiling blood, circumscribes the desert. Nardo's Phlegethon divides the Blasphemous from the others under the searing rain.

Botticelli's drawing for Canto 14 is missing, but the 1481 plate derived from it is quite animated. The Capaneus of the Yates-Thompson MS, if it be he talking to Dante and Virgil at the left, is hardly expressive of Dante's character, nor do the Sodomites at the right seem particularly in pain. The 1544 has the burning plain surrounded by the Wood of the Suicides. Dante and Virgil first encounter the Old Man of Crete at the right middle. The top half of the inner circle contains the Blasphemers and Capaneus, the lower left quadrant has the Sodomites, the lower right the Usurers, Phlegethon coursing between the two.

Blake's Sodomites have flames at their genitals, the Blasphemers and Usurers are lightly penciled in at the lower left corner. Doré's depiction of the whole scene is full of intense agony, Capaneus presumably the figure with raised arm and clenched fist at the lower left. Scaramuzza's Capaneus expresses the *superbia* (pride) of Dante's lines 60–63, while Mazza's the *rabbia* and *furor* (rage and fury).

Vatican, Biblioteca Apostolica, MS lat. 4776 (Florentine, ca. 1390–1400).

Paris, Bibliothèque Nationale, MS. it. 74 (Florentine, Bartolomeo di Fruosino, ca. 1420).

186

London, British Museum, Yates Thompson MS 36 (Priamo della Quercia, mid-fifteenth century).

1481 ed., Florence, copperplate engraving.

187

*William Blake, 1825–27, watercolor, National Gallery of
Victoria.*

William Blake 1825–27, watercolor, Fogg Gallery.

Gustave Doré, 1861, engraving of drawing.

Francesco Scaramuzza, 1865, pen drawing.

Emma Mazza, 1956 ed., Turin.

192

15

CANTO DECIMOQVINTO.

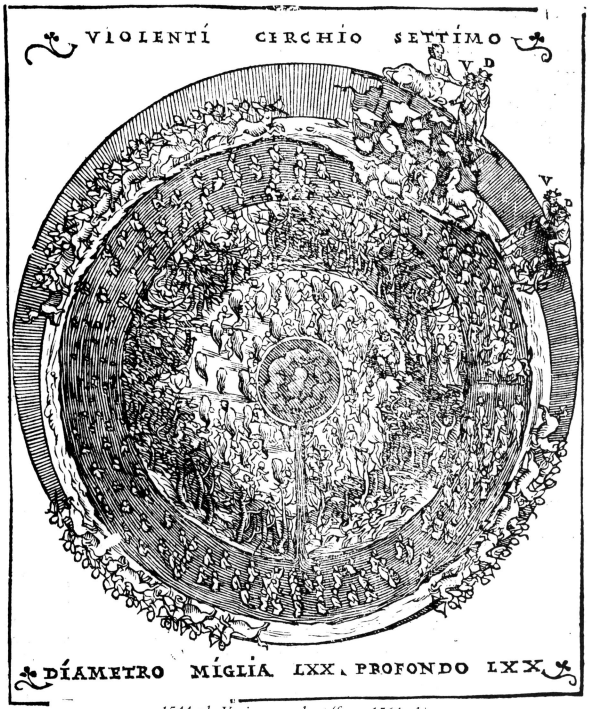

1544 ed., Venice, woodcut (from 1564 ed.).

Canto 15

Dante's encounter with Brunetto Latini and the three noble Florentines demonstrate his pain in learning of the sin of sodomy in men he had considered admirable leaders, scholars, and teachers. Ser Brunetto Latini is addressed as *voi* (as was Farinata degli Uberti), called a "radiance among men" and a "winner". The Yates-Thompson miniature (mentioned in the Introduction) has very touching expressions on the Dante with bowed head, depicted twice. The bearded Latini walks with Dante in the middle sequence of the illumination; presumably one of the three Florentines holds the hem of Dante's cloak in the left sequence, though it is Latini who does so in Dante's text. The miniature is, however, true to the spirit of the text, if not to the letter. Equally touching is the early miniature in the Florentine MS in the Biblioteca Nazionale, MS Palat. 313, with Dante holding the hand of the melancholy Latini. The Vat. 4776 miniature attempts to capture a benign quality in Dante's beloved former teacher. The Vat. 365's Dante is properly respectful, though Latini seems much younger than in Dante's description. The landscape once again is hardly Dante's; Latini is burned by the flakes of flame.

The Botticelli is a rare instance in his drawings of an almost-completed painting, done curiously from a sort of aerial view, with Dante and Virgil walking above the burning plain on which the Sodomites endlessly pace. Latini appears three times, first touching the hem of Dante's garment at the upper left corner, then, just below, conversing with the bowed Dante, finally saying farewell at the lower left. Latini's expressions in the first two instances are masterfully done, as are those of the contorted sinners under the rain of fire, though the whole composition is not so pleasing as the details.

The Dante and Latini expressions in the Flaxman are effective, unusually so for Flaxman's rather detached, abstracting style.

194

Florence, Biblioteca Nazionale, MS Palat. 313 (Florentine, ca. 1330s).

Vatican Biblioteca Apostolica, MS lat. 4776 (Florentine, ca. 1390–1400).

London, British Museum, Yates Thompson MS 36 (Priamo della Quercia, mid-fifteenth century).

Vatican Biblioteca Apostolica, MS Urb. lat. 365 (Gugliel-mo Giraldi & assistants, ca. 1478).

Sandro Botticelli, ca. 1478, Biblioteca Apostolica Vaticana.

John Flaxman, 1793, engraving of drawing.

16

CANTO DECIMOSESTO.

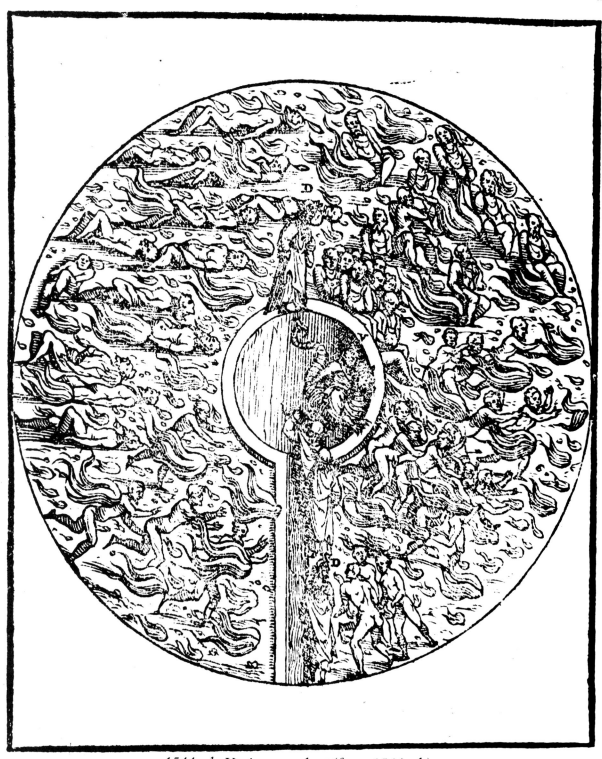

1544 ed., Venice, woodcut (from 1564 ed.)

Canto 16

The three noble Florentines punished eternally for sodomy (homosexuality) have proven intriguing to illustrators. Their punishment includes not only the rain of fire and the ceaseless movement, but also an endless circling dance together, presumably symbolizing to Dante the barren circle of homosexual union. Their roundelays are compared by Dante to the grappling of male wrestlers, but to different, sinful ends. And yet both Dante and Virgil deeply respect the three. Dante would throw himself down into the lower plain to embrace these men out of compassion and affection. Virgil, introducing them, says "these are men to whom respect is due . . . it were more fitting you ran after them." This complex body of conflicting attitudes in Dante, as in the case of Brunetto Latini, deserves a subtle rendering. The scene, in fact, has fared better with illustrators than the Latini.

The Chantilly illumination captures a grace and poignancy in the sinners, the Vat. 4776 the grotesqueness of the punishment. The Fruosino has a sardonic touch typical of his illustrations. The Florentine MS. (Laurenziana Plut. 40.1) has the Sodomites arm in arm, not quite accurate to Dante though appropriate, and scarred by flames, quite as Dante describes.

The Botticelli drawing has the three Florentines circling tortuously in the upper left corner. The bottom half of the drawing moves on to the lower escarpment, where the Usurers crouch with purses about their necks. Dante removes a cord about his waist with which to summon the monster of Fraud, Geryon, who appears at the bottom left. The 1481 plate shows more independence than usual from the Botticelli, focusing at the center the three Sodomites, here depicted without grace, simply with shame and torment, and with fire at the groin. The Stradanus is equally grim, with the claustrophobic tightness of the sinners and the overall darkness. The Flaxman succeeds in conveying the agony of the circling dancers; one wishes the Dante and Virgil expressions had also added something to the tone of the whole. Koch's hot-footed dancers convey the pain, but little of the dignity of the Florentines.

Blake's Dante conveys the appropriate compassion. The whirling Florentines recall the flow of illicit lovers of Blake's illustration for Canto 5, though in this case the lust is circular; in the Canto 5 illustration it is an endlessly flowing wave. Holm's running figures against the barren white space convey Dante's sense of the sterility of their sin and the starkness of their punishment.

rt de qbr autor interrogauit Ciacchu ut hi
Patrus mitio circulo.cantu.vi.

frīs tau clamat ad me de tīa . Et de sodomi
tis ait ad abraā . clamoz sodomoz uenit

Chantilly, Musée Conde, MS 597 (Pisan, ca. 1345).

Vatican, Biblioteca Apostolica, MS lat. 4776 (Florentine, ca. 1390–1400).

Paris, Bibliothèque Nationale, MS it. 74 (Florentine, Bartolomeo di Fruosino, ca. 1420).

Florence, Biblioteca Laurenziana, MS Plut. 40.1 (North Italian, 1456).

*Sandro Botticelli, ca. 1478, Biblioteca Apostolica Vat-
icana.*

1481 ed., Florence, copperplate engraving.

204

Stradanus (Jan van der Straet) 1587, Laurentian Library,
Florence.

John Flaxman, 1793, engraving of drawing.

Joseph Anton Koch, ca. 1803–25, pen drawing.

William Blake 1825–27, watercolor, Fogg Gallery.

Ebba Holm, 1929, woodcut.

17

CANTO DECIMOSETTIMO.

1544 ed., Venice, woodcut (from 1564 ed.).

Canto 17

The high comedy of the Usurers saving places for like brethren still alive on earth (who presumably read of their coming fate!) is largely missing in the tonalities of the illustrations. The gigantic purses emblazoned with family coats-of-arms and hanging from the necks of the Usurers in the British Museum Egerton manuscript is perhaps intended as sardonic; the Baskin with the jaded faces is certainly intended so. The Fruosino from whom we expect irony has, disappointingly, his Usurers without purses and simply miserable in expression, not at all sarcastic, as in the text. Botticelli's Usurers have the purses around their necks, but without the coats-of-arms. perhaps the 1481 engraving handles the Usurers best of all.

The Geryon monster of the 1481 is clearly derived from the Botticelli, but it adds a crown on the head of the "beast who makes the whole world stink." Botticelli's Geryon beautifully captures Dante's description of Fraud's fair, false face, the body both hairy and serpentine (elaborately patterned), and the tail with scorpion sting. The 1544 woodcut changes half-way down the drawing from an effective rendering of space, as the Geryon monster circles downward, to a diagrammatic depiction of the ten *malebolge* to come in the succeeding cantos. Flaxman's Geryon is quite pedestrian, though the fear and trepidation of Dante and Virgil is well done; not so well, however, as the Koch. Doré's depiction is most effective, Dante and Virgil cowering on Geryon's back, the Inferno landscape below terrifying. The Vat. 4776 miniature renders a sense of wonder, as Dante proceeds into the *malebolge* with an air of expectation.

London, British Museum, Egerton MS 943 (Emilian or Paduan, second quarter of fourteenth century).

Vatican, Biblioteca Apostolica, MS lat. 4776 (Florentine, ca. 1390–1400).

212

Paris, Bibliothèque Nationale, MS. it. 74 (Florentine, Bartolomeo di Fruosino, ca. 1420).

Sandro Botticelli, ca. 1478, Kupferstichkabinett, Staatliche Museen, Preussischer Kulturbesitz, Berlin.

1481 ed., Florence, copperplate engraving.

John Flaxman, 1793, engraving of drawing.

214

Joseph Anton Koch, ca. 1825, fresco.

Gustave Doré, 1861, engraving of drawing.

216

Leonard Baskin, 1969 ed., New York.

18

CANTO DECIMOOTTAVO.

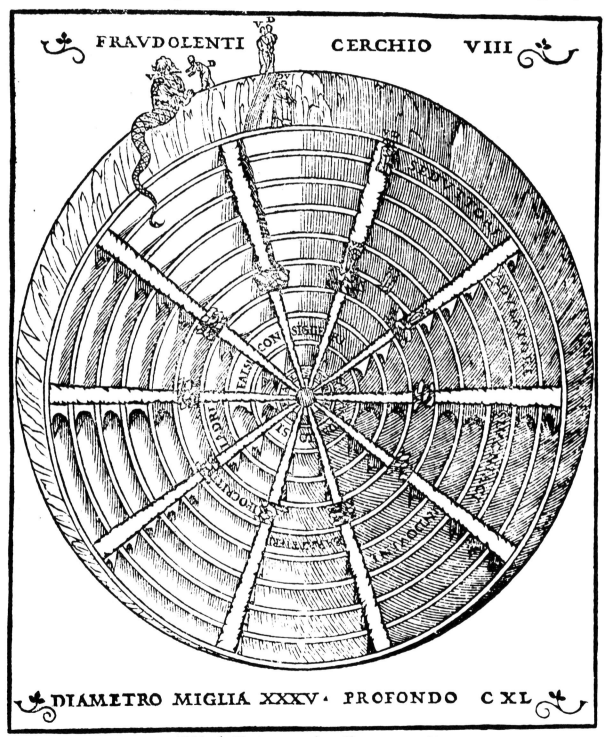

1544 ed., Venice, woodcut (from 1564 ed.).

Canto 18

The Manfredini effectively evokes the *malebolge* to come, the ten vast concentric gullies of the Fraudulent. Vat. 4776 does not have the Panderers and Seducers moving by one another (goaded by devils) as in Dante's text, but rather confronting one another, much as Vat. 4776's depiction of the Hoarders and Wasters of Canto 7. The Nardo fresco (Spec. Sec.) depicts only one of the two groups, and the Vat. 4776 artist, so often influenced by the Nardo, seems to have added the second group as he would prefer to have them. The animal head on the second devil, left, occurs in some of Botticelli's devils and was traditional in devil presentations. The Vat. 365 miniature is a beautiful composition, but as usual for the artist, the punishments of Hell are humanistically modulated to a rather bearable unpleasantness. The devils wield their goads in the Fruosino with an energy typical of the sardonic nature of the artist, who therewith captures a tonality in Dante often missed by other illustrators.

Botticelli's Thais, at the lower middle of the painting, is sardonic and effective. Blake's Thais is beautiful, as is Guttuso's, but there is humor in the Guttuso (for all of the tormenting itch) quite absent in the Blake. Blake has, at the upper left of his drawing, either a Panderer or a Seducer being chased by a flying female with a goad in her hand. This divergence from Dante is a clear indication of a personal statement of Blake's concerning female seductions, a statement of which the Thais figure is likely a part.

The Lombard miniature has Dante on the bridge between *bolge* overcome by the stench from the Flatterers, who are appropriately scratching, grimacing, or wallowing, as also in the Botticelli, the Stradanus, the Zuccaro, the Flaxman, and the Koch (Stradanus's rendition is particularly nauseating). Botticelli's drawing (completely colored except for the Geryon at the upper left corner) is remarkably animated. Among the Seducers at the middle right is Jason who wears a crown, but Botticelli does not otherwise render Dante's "great soul" who sheds no tears and moves with "kingliness . . . even in Hell". (It is an opportunity missed by all of the illustrations herein presented.) Among the Flatterers, Alessio Interminelli, speaking to Dante at the lower right corner, is magnificently drawn. (Above, among the Panderers, Caccianemico hides his head in speaking to Dante; the devil next to him has both a male and female nature.) The 1481 engraving is confused in having the Panderers and Seducers submerged rather than fleeing, but their gestures and expressions of suffering are moving, presumably influenced by the Botticelli.

219

Vatican, Biblioteca Apostolica, MS lat. 4776 (Florentine, ca. 1390–1400).

Paris, Bibliothèque Nationale, MS it. 2017 (Lombard, ca. 1440).

*Vatican, Biblioteca Apostolica, MS Urb. lat. 365
(Guglielmo Giraldi & assistants, ca. 1478).*

*Sandro Botticelli, ca. 1478, Kupferstichkabinett, Staat-
liche Museen, Preussischer Kulturbesitz, Berlin.*

1481 ed., Florence, copperplate engraving.

*Stradanus (Jan van der Straet) 1587, Laurentian Library,
Florence.*

John Flaxman, 1793, engraving of drawing.

Joseph Anton Koch, ca. 1803–25, pen drawing.

William Blake, 1825–27, watercolor, Fogg Gallery.

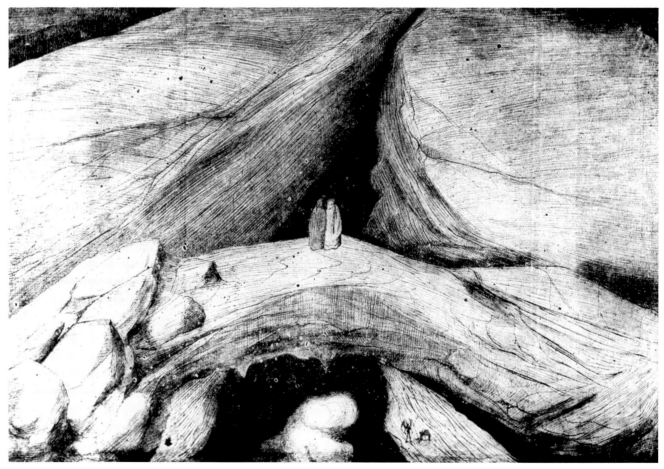

Manfredo Manfredini, 1907, engraving of drawing.

Renato Guttuso, 1969 ed., Rome.

227

CANTO DECIMONONO.

1544 ed., Venice, woodcut (from 1564 ed.).

19

Canto 19

The Simonists are those who make profit from religion; that is, who turn religion upside down. Dante has a perfect ironic punishment for these, as they burn eternally in hell upside down in round holes in the *bolgia* floor. Dante stresses the comic irony by comparing the burning holes to baptismal fonts. The Naples illustration, in fact, depicts the typical font of the day. Vatican 4776, following the Nardo fresco (Spec. Sec.), suggests a font by its raised conical holes, while the earlier Palatine MS depicts the holes more literally, Dante bending, as the text says, as if he were hearing the confession of the sinner. He, in fact, is listening to Pope Nicholas III, who, in a passage of great comedy, has been expecting the arrival of the succeeding Pope, Boniface VIII, while also predicting the eventual coming of the Pope after Boniface, Clement V! The comedic aspects of the Canto are stressed, perhaps inevitably, given the nature of the imagery, in most illustrations to the Canto.

Botticelli especially emphasizes the gross obscenity of God's servants as profiteers (and perhaps alluding to the sexual nature of Dante's comparison of a usurous Church to the Whore of Babylon) by having the Simonists' sexual organs exposed, though Dante has them submerged in flame to mid-thigh. One Simonist, just above center and to the left, is not upside down or submerged, but rather appears to be shoring up the wall between him and the Flatterers. Virgil is pictured carrying Dante down into the *bolgia* and then up again. The 1481 engraving has the Dante and Virgil return trip squeezed into the lower right corner and has the Simonists submerged lower into the ground. Zuccaro focuses on Virgil carrying Dante down the steep slope.

Blake, in a powerful drawing, diverges from Dante in having Pope Nicholas's flaming tomb within a cave, symbolizing in Blake's system spiritual and perceptual deprivation. Dante being carried by Virgil is perhaps a bit too terrified to represent the Dante who magnificently berates the Pope and Usury in lines 82–115. The Pinelli has Dante rather more in charge.

229

*Florence, Biblioteca Nazionale, MS Palat. 313 (Florentine,
ca. 1330s).*

Vatican, Biblioteca Apostolica, MS lat. 4776 (Florentine, ca. 1390–1400).

Naples, Biblioteca Girolamini, MS C.F.4.20 (Central or South Italian, third quarter of fourteenth century).

*Sandro Botticelli, ca. 1478, Kupferstichkabinett, Staat-
liche Museen, Preussischer Kulturbesitz, Berlin.*

1481 ed. Florence, copperplate engraving.

Federico Zuccaro, ca. 1587, Uffizi, Florence.

Bartolomeo Pinelli, 1826, engraving of drawing.

William Blake 1825–27, watercolor, Tate Gallery.

20

1544 ed., Venice, woodcut (from 1564 ed.).

Canto 20

The Diviners are those who in the past have been so presumptuous as to predict the future (which is in God's hands) and who are punished in Hell by having their heads on backwards, unable even to see where they are walking. The eternal procession is described by Dante as deeply sad, a "dark desolation" in which each sinner is "bathed in tears," a parade so sorrowful that Dante himself weeps, rebuked then by Virgil. This somber mood ought to be caught by the illustrator.

Vatican 4776 (borrowing some motifs from the Nardo fresco) manages the compassion of Dante, the reproval by Virgil, and the pathos of the Diviners. The figure on the ground is presumably Amphiareus, who fell to the ground at Thebes. The lady of the long tresses is certainly Manto, as she is described in lines 52–65. The bearded figure is probably Eurypylus, the Greek auger of lines 106–14. Eurypylus and Manto are the only figures discernible in the Botticelli. While Dante's compassion and Virgil's detachment are clear in the upper vignette in the Botticelli, the somber mood of the Diviners' procession is hardly rendered, the *bolgia* being too light and open. Certainly the landscape of the 1747 edition is too charming, with the high, cloudy sky. The Diviners here are without much dignity, largely a freak show, though the bending figure staring upwards is an ingenious idea.

Blake's Dante and Virgil are barely sketched in, but it seems Blake intended to show Virgil detached and Dante compassionate, with Dante's arm on his knee and his head on his arm. The Diviners are draped, perhaps to show some respect on Blake's part for the prophetic impulse. Manto is beautiful with fillets in her hair. The male prophets (one quite reminiscent of Blake's recurrent Urizen figure) are closed in by the bridge and smoke, much as in the confining cave of the Simonists of the previous canto.

Stassen's *Art Nouveau* style is often lightweight in interpretive power of Dante, but in his drawing for Canto 20 he manages, with his effective line and his beautiful nudes, to convey a sense of dignity and pathos to these ancient prophets, a sense of sad constriction in the movements of those who once pretended to have the universe in their field of vision.

Holm's endless narrow and circular procession hard by a cliffside, with Dante weeping high above, catches Dante's tonality, though the Diviners can scarcely be distinguished. Mazza effectively funnels the Soothsayers through a narrow, dark space, representative of the sinners' total loss of vision: they appear as both prisoners and zombies. Baskin's Tiresias weeps from his blind eyes, and the tears flow (as Dante says) in a rivulet down the cleft of his back: a fine example of a Dante symbol finding a harmony within a modern consciousness.

Florence, Biblioteca Nazionale, MS Palat. 313 (Florentine, ca. 1330s).

Vatican, Biblioteca Apostolica, MS lat. 4776 (Florentine, ca. 1390–1400).

Sandro Botticelli, ca. 1478, Kupferstichkabinett, Staatliche Museen, Preussischer Kulturbesitz, Berlin.

1757 ed., Venice, engraving.

William Blake, 1825–27, watercolor, National Gallery of
Victoria.

241

XX.

Verrenkte Leiber ſah ich dann mit Grauen.
 Es war der Zukunftskünder Strafgericht.
Den Sehern, Zaubrern, Männern ſowie Frauen,
 Stand überm nackten Rücken das Geſicht:
Die Allmacht ſtrafte ſo ihr Vorwärtsſchauen.
 Der Meiſter ſprach, das Hören ward zur Pflicht,
Und ſo erfuhr ich, was die Sage kündet
Von Manto, die ſein Mantua gegründet.

Franz Stassen, 1906, pen and ink drawing.

Ebba Holm, 1929, woodcut.

243

Emma Mazza, 1956 ed., Turin.

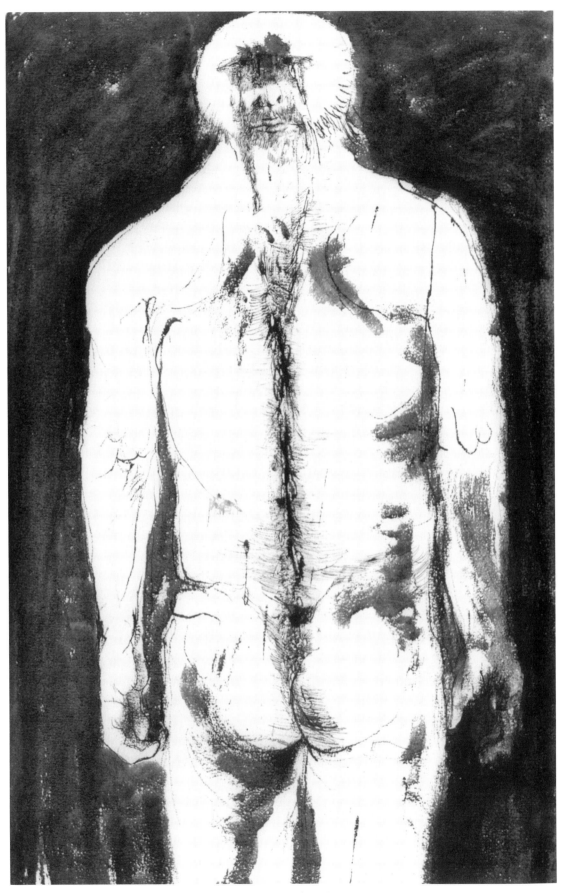

Leonard Baskin, 1969 ed., New York.

245

21

CANTO VENTESIMOPRIMO.

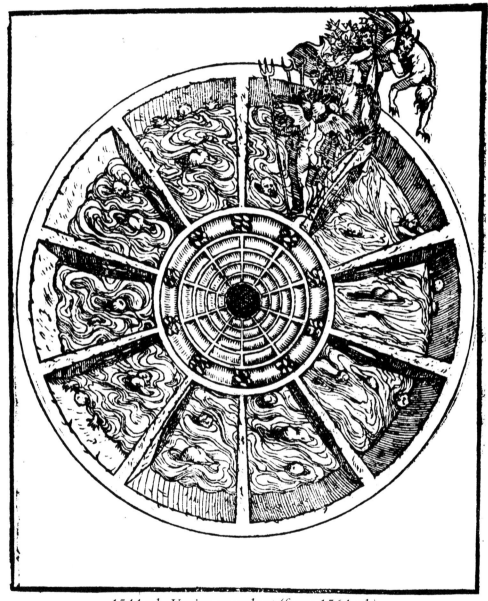

1544 ed., Venice, woodcut (from 1564 ed.).

22

CANTO VENTESIMOSECONDO.

1544 ed., Venice, woodcut (from 1564 ed.).

Cantos 21–22

Cantos 21 and 22 are both concerned with Grafters, appropriately punished by submersion in boiling pitch. Both Cantos are, tonally, savage burlesque, dealing mainly with political graft, of which Dante himself had been accused. His accusers are perhaps satirized in the malicious devils (their leader Malacoda, or "Bad-ass"). Dante's sense of the endemic nature of graft in Northern Italy of his time is symbolized in the remarks about Lucca ("everyone there is a grafter . . . / There 'Yes' is 'No' and 'No' is 'Yes' for a fee") and in the vignette of the Navarrese, who betrays his comrades in the pitch to make his own escape. Dante the character fears the devils; Dante the author scorns them and plays them for ironic comedy.

The Chantilly parade of devils (ll. 118–25) is a spoof on the devils' comic militarism, their heads marvelously grotesque. Vatican 4776's devils have the head and feet of various animals (Botticelli's have, in addition, female breasts and male sexual organs). In the Fruosino two of the Grafters are obviously tonsured. The Angelica miniature depicts (1) the carrying of a magistrate of Lucca by a devil above the river of pitch, (2) Virgil admonishing the devils while Dante cowers behind a bridge, and (3) the Grafters immersed in the river. Vatican 4776 has in its lower half the anonymous Navarrese fleeing the two fighting devils. Fruosino has the Navarrese impaled above a pool of pitch while the Laurenziana has three Grafters impaled above an ornate bridge, one presumably the Navarrese with his arm detached.

Botticelli's first plate, read serially from the upper left in a backward "s" direction to the lower right, has the Grafter of Lucca falling into the pitch, Dante fearful at the bridge there, then cowering lower left, Virgil negotiating lower center, and finally a devil breaking wind at the lower right. (The Palatine miniature reads Dante too literally, having one of the devils with a trumpet at his behind.) The second Botticelli plate, with the Flatterers in their *bolgia* at the upper half, has the grotesque parade at the lower left, the Navarrese first on the ground, then diving back into the pitch, the devils fighting amongst themselves center right. The burlesque tone of the Botticelli drawings for these two cantos is everywhere appropriate.

The 1544 woodcut provides a diagram of the Grafters' *bolgia* with its sticky pitch, and then the next six *bolge;* the magistrate of Lucca is held aloft at the top right corner. Flaxman, Ademolli, Blake, and Scaramuzza all similarly render the Lucca vignette, Ademolli's devil more furry than the others. Doré's plates effectively capture the wild scramble, the malice, and the buffoonery of the devils.

Blake's engraving of the Navarrese vignette has the victim so handsome, the rip at the flesh so shocking, and the four devils so repellant that one cannot help feeling that Blake has a personal stake here well beyond the depiction of a traitorous and slippery Grafter getting his due. The flower motif on the stone, on which one devil sits, adds to the ambiguous tone of the piece. Blake's fighting devils have more of the simple, stupid malice of Dante's description. The Manfredini perhaps captures best the Navarrese vignette, in the rather lean, rat-or-bat-like nature of both Grafter and devils.

Ecunffelfiu chemipuc uua lorm. Lontm
e quordam aual longum gmeale asbule
feu du atq; mgru qusaus i foueis aquatei
e foffaris. Huie itaqaiali auto opar na
uarrenfe.

Aiamadre affuo du signor mpofe
chemauea geneiuro dun ribaldo
diftrugitor dife i difue cofe. Ht traate demmt
q diffiu fir ir bamttatore i nbaldu. Bamr
tator e fe e qrolo ul frmide o republica ut
yconomica y pecunia aligd opar. Ribal

quagenari peffs. L. hoibz Sub qui quaqe
nario u pofuit v. decanos fiu decun oes ut
qlz iftor v. preeffer v. Orta u lite ir x. fin
bant aduidicau decam. eu facile emr lite
paucor diune. Sz fino potant lite diffir
decai ibat ad qnqgenam. Or qnqgenam
ar adcetunone. Cetuno ad tbunu. Si tri
bun uo lite deimmae no potur ibat ad mo
ufen qenat qi monacha populi.

Su fratre gomita. Ifte fr Gomita fuir de reg
Sardime. Or cu cer iudieatu gallun uicai

Chantilly, Museé Conde, MS 597 (Pisan, ca. 1345).

*Vatican Biblioteca Apostolica, MS lat. 4776 (Florentine,
ca. 1390–1400).*

249

Vatican, Biblioteca Apostolica, MS lat. 4776 (Florentine, ca. 1390–1400).

Rome, Biblioteca Angelica, MS 1102 (Bolognese, early fifteenth century).

Sandro Botticelli, ca. 1478, Kupferstichkabinett, Staatliche Museen, Preussischer Kulturbesitz, Berlin.

John Flaxman, 1793, engraving of drawing.

Luigi Ademolli, 1817, engraving of drawing.

252

William Blake, 1825–27, watercolor, National Gallery of Victoria.

Gustave Doré, 1861, engraving of drawing.

Gustave Doré, 1861, engraving of drawing.

Francesco Scaramuzza, 1865, pen drawing.

*Florence, Biblioteca Nazionale, MS Palat. 313 (Florentine,
ca. 1330s).*

Vatican, Biblioteca Apostolica, MS lat. 4776 (Florentine, ca. 1390–1400).

Paris, Bibliothèque Nationale, MS. it. 74 (Florentine, Bartolomeo di Fruosino, ca. 1420).

ordinatione e distontio. Equi pone fine al
predetto capitolo.

Canto xxiij. nel quale si abhomina q̃l-
li et tratta alchuna cossa della sagaci-
tade delli barattieri.

I Quidi gia cavalicar movie capo
e comenzar storno e far lor mostra.
e tal volta fugire p̃ lo scampo.
Contra vidi per la tra nostra.
fo aretini e vidi gir gualdaine.
e se dir tornamenti e corer giostra.
h Quado co trobe e quado co campane.
co tabari e g̃ cong di costella.
k e co messe nostrali o cose istraine.

Florence, Biblioteca Laurenziana, MS Plut. 40.1 (North
Italian, 1456).

260

*Sandro Botticelli, ca. 1478, Kupferstichkabinett, Staat-
liche Museen, Preussischer Kulturbesitz, Berlin.*

261

William Blake, 1825–27, watercolor, Fogg Gallery.

William Blake 1825–27, watercolor, Birmingham Art Gallery.

Manfredo Manfredini, 1907, engraving of drawing.

23

CANTO VENTESIMOTERZO.

1544 ed., Venice woodcut (from 1564 ed.)

Canto 23

Dante's symbolic punishment for the Hypocrites is so rich and suggestive that it has inspired some of the very best illustrative art. The outwardly brilliant coat of lead is the burden of one's hypocrisy; the hypocrite trudges along forever under the weight of his own disguises. Dante has the Hypocrites "moaning in misery" with "floods of tears that drown their cheeks." The expressions on the faces of the Hypocrites in the two Parisian manuscripts—the Lombard and the Fruosino—are deeply moving and absolutely right for Dante's canto. The Egerton manuscript in the British Museum, of almost a century earlier, anticipates the Lombard miniature, cruder in execution and expression, but with real power. Caiaphas, the Pharisee, who rationalized the crucifixion of Christ, is in each miniature sighing and suffering on his own cross, bearing the weight of the Hypocrites' tread.

The Botticelli rendering is not as effective as any of the three miniatures. Presumably it is Caiaphas at the lower left corner lying prone in the opposite direction to Annas and the other Pharisees (one wonders about Botticelli's reason for the hand-someness of Caiaphas's immediate neighbor at the stake). The devils who threaten Virgil (who is escaping down the slope bearing Dante in his arms) occupy the top half of the drawing, which, as a whole, while beautifully drawn in details, seems too fragmented and undramatic. As often, the 1544 woodcut seems to be a schematizing in a circular design of the Botticellian motifs.

Flaxman's first plate seems rather routine and uninspired; one certainly must question the good looks of the most prominent devil with the streaming hair, given the gargoyle descriptions of Dante's devils. Flaxman's second plate has succeeded in enormously influencing subsequent art, especially through Goya (see Bibliography: Symmonds). Flaxman's hooded figures through their simplified abstraction convey an intriguing sense of mystery, but Dante's Hypocrites are anything but mysterious. The Flaxman is then not so illustrative of Dante's attitudes as are the miniatures, though tantalizing, even profound, in its ambiguity.

Blake, while praising his friend Flaxman's Dante drawings, felt that his influence on Flaxman had not been sufficiently acknowledged. His Hypocrites are far more bowed down with suffering, perhaps as a consequence less ambiguous than Flax-man's. Blake's Caiaphas is clearly his Urizen figure. The threatening devils at the top of the drawing add little to the unfinished composition, but the slow march of the Hypocrites is magnificently rendered.

The Doré composition is similar to the Blake, though Doré's somber landscape and the endless train of the Hypocrites strike one as more Dantean than the Blake. The Dargent, as always derived from Doré, has an appropriate atmosphere, but the Caiaphas figure is perhaps too sculptured, too roundly anatomical to make any point other than the reality of pain. The Holm, a good deal like the Flaxman in its stylized simplicity, effectively conveys a sense of rhythmic pain for the sinners by the three groupings of Hypocrites in the near, middle, and far distance.

London, British Museum, Egerton MS 943 (Emilian or Paduan, second quarter of fourteenth century.

Paris, Bibliothèque Nationale, MS. it. 74 (Florentine, Bartolomeo di Fruosino, ca. 1420).

Paris, Bibliothèque Nationale, MS it. 2017 (Lombard, ca. 1440).

Sandro Botticelli, ca. 1478, Kupferstichkabinett, Staatliche Museen, Preussischer Kulturbesitz, Berlin.

John Flaxman, 1793, engraving of drawing.

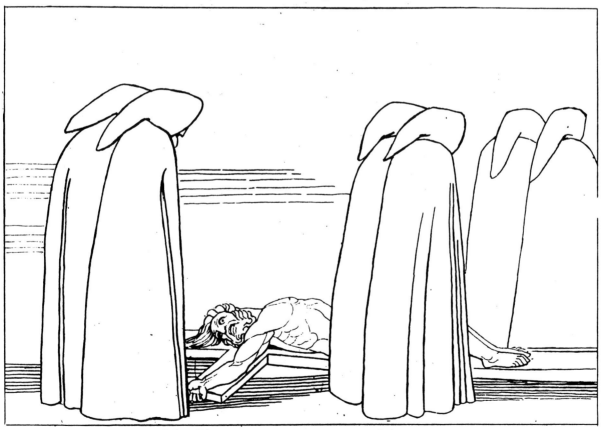

John Flaxman, 1793, engraving of drawing.

William Blake, 1825–27, watercolor, Tate Gallery.

Gustave Doré, 1861, engraving of drawing.

Yan Dargent, 1879, engraving of drawing.

Ebba Holm, 1929, woodcut.

273

24

CANTO VENTESIMOQVARTO.

1544, ed., Venice, woodcut (from 1564 ed.).

25

CANTO VENTESIMOQVINTO.

1544 ed., Venice, woodcut (from 1564 ed.).

Cantos 24–25

Snake (and dragon) motifs in the punishment of sinners are, of course, of ancient origin, and in Medieval and early Renaissance "Last Judgments" reptiles are customarily used throughout as binding and biting agents. See the Baptistery mosaic, the Giotto, the Traini, the Bartolo, the Giovanni da Modena, and the Fra Angelico frescos all in the Special Section, and the magnificent detail of the bas-relief of Lorenzo Maitani at the Cathedral at Orvieto.

Dante's snakes and dragons punish specifically the Thieves, their stealth, and deception; Dante adds the brilliant metamorphosis idea wherein thief turns into snake and snake into thief, with thief-changed-to-snake biting another thief to regain human form temporarily. Dante boasts he has bested Ovid in the allegoric use of the metamorphic idea, and so he has. In Canto 25 one looks especially for illustrators who handle, and how well they handle, these metamorphoses.

The Nardo fresco beautifully illustrates two of the major motifs of the snake cantos: the Centaur Caucus with snakes in his hands and a dragon on his back, and Vanni Fucci, the thief of the Sacristy, snake-entangled, sending up an obscene gesture to God. The illustration is largely copied by Vat. 4776 (first plate), with the usual addition of the Dante and Virgil figures. The Fruosino is likewise derived from the Nardo. Vat. 4776 (second plate) has a dragon biting the prone Fucci on the neck, burning him to dust, before he returns to human form again. The Paduan miniature captures the same moment, the flame and smoke of the incineration of Fucci surrounding him.

The Fruosino (second plate) has the thieves in a circular snake pit (similar to the circle in the Traini fresco in the Special Section); the six-footed dragon with the human face is the beast who bites Cianfa in Canto 25 and is in the process of taking on human shape.

The first Botticelli depicts in the upper half of the drawing the arduous climb up and down to the *bolgia* of the Thieves and the conversation of Dante and Virgil with Vanni Fucci at the bottom center. Fucci in flames is pictured just to the left. The thieves, the snakes, and the dragons are all beautifully drawn, though one looks in vain in Botticelli's drawings for Cantos 24–5 for renditions of the thieves in the process of metamorphosing into reptiles, the motif of which Dante was justifiably proud.

The 1757 has an effectively drawn central figure writhing on the rock. Flaxman's study is largely academic. Dargent's vast crowd of serpents and thieves is a rare example of this disciple of Doré's managing a more awesome scene than his master, though Dante describes no such crowd. Guttuso, discussed earlier in the Introduction, may have been influenced by the Dargent in his drawing which is similarly crowded, though certainly more whimsical.

The Chantilly miniatures depict a serpent attacking Buoso and then the mid-stage of metamorphosis of one into the other; together they are perhaps the best rendition of Dante's effect. The second Botticelli includes Cacus, Agnello Brunelleschi attacked by the six-footed serpent, and Vanni Fucci "making figs" at God.

Blake's Fucci, much like his Capaneus (with whom Fucci is compared by Dante), has charisma, again implying Blake's admiration for the natural rebel against

276

institutional religion, despicable thief though Fucci may be. Brunelleschi's head being swallowed by the serpent (sometimes Cianfa) and the subsequent plate of Brunelleschi half transformed into a serpent are magnificent renditions of Dante's horrific and masterful allegories.

Koch's Brunelleschi and the serpent is perhaps his finest illustration to Dante; Stassen's is perhaps derivative of Koch's. Ademolli's Cacus and Agnello are less energetic or fearsome than some others, though Agnello half transformed to a snake has strength.

The Lebruns have a man first being crushed and then limp from the snake's force, both powerful symbols of Lebrun's sense of a modern helplessness, both conveying at the same time a sense of Dantean compassion.

Lorenzo Maitani, facade, Orvieto Cathedral, ca. 1320.

Vatican, Biblioteca Apostolica,
MS lat. 4776 (Florentine, ca. 1390–1400).

Padua, Biblioteca del Seminario, MS 67 (Padua, early fif-
teenth century).

278

Paris, Bibliothèque Nationale, MS.it. 74 (Florentine, Bartolomeo di Fruosino, ca. 1420).

Sandro Botticelli, ca. 1478, Kupferstichkabinett, Staatliche Museen, Preussischer Kulturbesitz, Berlin.

279

1757 ed., Venice, engraving.

280

John Flaxman, 1793, engraving of drawing.

Yan Dargent, 1879, engraving of drawing.

Renato Guttuso, 1969, ed. Rome.

chenoe nero ancor elbiancomore
Lialtin due nguardauan eaascuno

longum uocatur. Oz incoruptu abign
fuatur e album. Oz uo cute rugofa et h

moeant in famem e putredmem fiunt

Chantilly, Musée Conde, MS 597 (Pisan, ca. 1345).

284

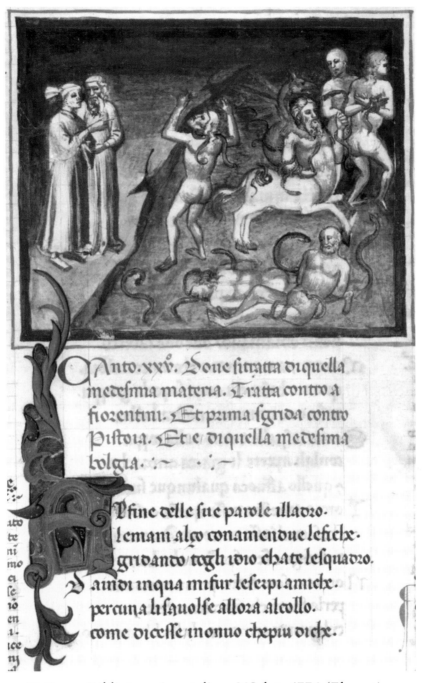

Canto. xxv. Doue sitratta diquella
medesima materia. Tratta contro a
fiorentini. Et prima segonda contro
Pistoia. Et e diquella medesima
bolgia.

Pfine delle sue parole illadro.
lemani alço conamendue lefiche.
gridando togli idio chate lesquadro.
Damdi inqua misfur leserpi amiche.
percina li sauolse alloza alcollo.
come dicesse innonuo chepiu diche.

Vatican, Biblioteca Apostolica, MS lat. 4776 (Florentine,
ca. 1390–1400).

285

Paris, Bibliothèque Nationale, MS. it. 74 (Florentine, Bartolomeo di Fruosino, ca. 1420).

Sandro Botticelli, ca. 1478, Kupferstichkabinett, Staatliche Museen, Preussischer Kulturbesitz, Berlin.

286

Luigi Ademolli, 1817, engraving of drawing.

William Blake, 1825–27, watercolor, National Gallery of Victoria.

William Blake, 1825–27, watercolor, National Gallery of Victoria.

William Blake, 1825–27, watercolor, Fogg Gallery.

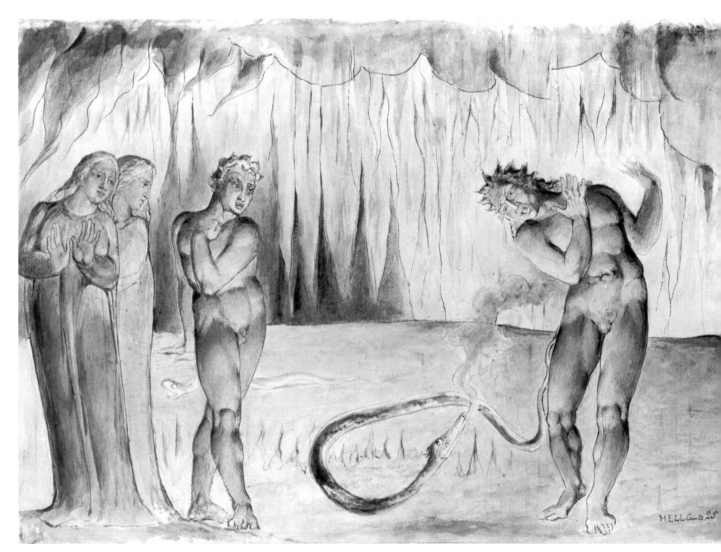

William Blake, 1825–27, watercolor, Tate Gallery.

Joseph Anton Koch, ca. 1803–25, pen drawing.

291

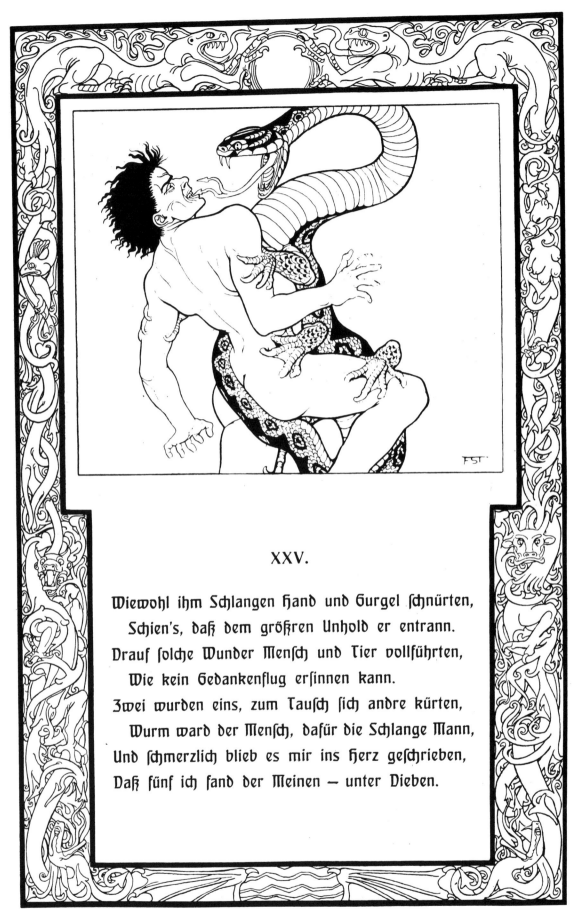

XXV.

Wiewohl ihm Schlangen Hand und Gurgel schnürten,
    Schien's, daß dem größren Unhold er entrann.
Drauf solche Wunder Mensch und Tier vollführten,
    Wie kein Gedankenflug ersinnen kann.
Zwei wurden eins, zum Tausch sich andre kürten,
    Wurm ward der Mensch, dafür die Schlange Mann,
Und schmerzlich blieb es mir ins Herz geschrieben,
    Daß fünf ich fand der Meinen — unter Dieben.

Franz Stassen, 1906, pen and ink drawing.

Rico Lebrun, 1962 ed., Northampton, Mass.

293

Rico Lebrun, 1962 ed., Northampton, Mass.

26

CANTO VENTESIMOSESTO.

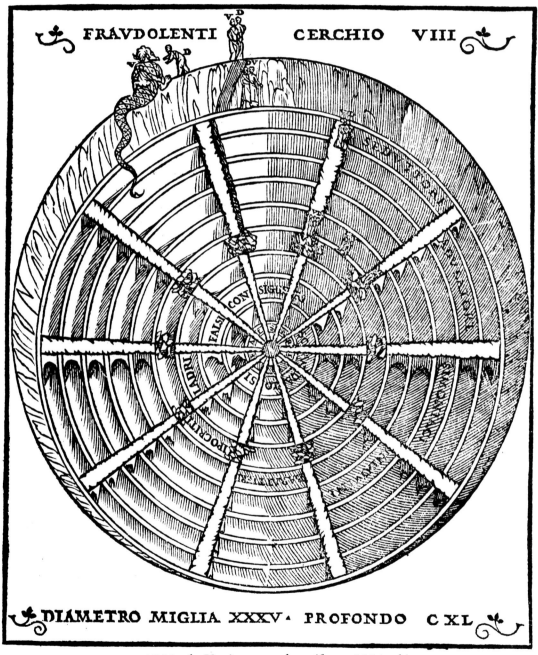

1544 ed., Venice, woodcut (from 1564 ed.).

27

CANTO VENTESIMOSETTIMO.

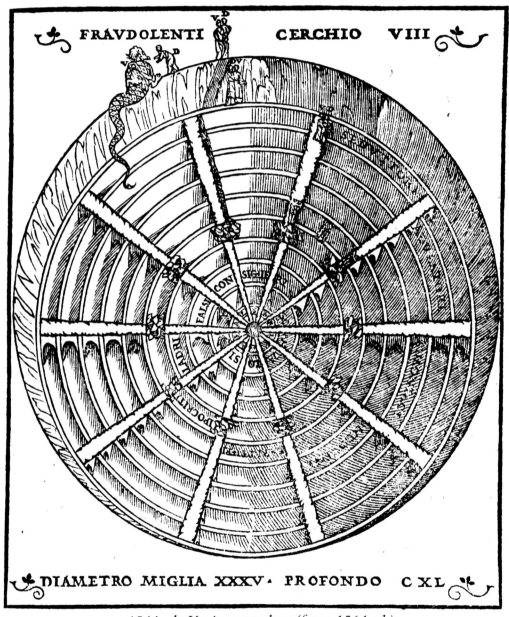

1544 ed., Venice, woodcut (from 1564 ed.).

Cantos 26–27

The "Evil Counselors" Cantos 26 and 27, where the sinners speak out of flames, have proven difficult to illustrate and caused many illustrators to depict rather the earthly history of the sinners than their state in Hell. Dante evokes awe through the suffering voices in the flame with no persons visible, but many of the illustrators have understandably felt impelled to give a visible embodiment to the voices. Thus, while in Vat. 4776 Ulysses and Diomede are clearly shown as co-conspirators sharing a double flame, their faces are barely sketched in the Botticelli; they are totally distinct in the Pinelli. Guido Da Montefeltro is fully depicted in the Vat. 4776; the Lombard miniature's (Spec. Sec.) flaming heads are more like Botticelli's.

Doré's marvelously atmospheric landscape dispenses with any depiction of figures out of the flames (as does the Holm, which is probably influenced by the Doré). Ulysses and Guido both are admired by Dante, though they both, of course, have chosen wrong paths that have brought them to Hell. The perilousness of human choice is symbolically depicted by the terrifying landscape of the Doré. Atmospherics and chiaroscuro in landscape become all-important in scenes such as this without human presences; the Botticellis are almost totally lacking these elements in the drawings for the two cantos. Pinelli's Dante and Virgil wedged in the rocks above the flames has animation; even the Holm conveys a sense of distance and space.

Many illustrators of these cantos have turned instead to the stirring recounting by Ulysses of his last journey to the end of the world, the Mount of Purgatory, and his subsequent shipwreck. The charming Vat. 4776 miniature of the shipwreck, while not really of Hell, is too good to omit. Likewise, the grimly comic scene of the soul of Guido being argued over by St. Francis and a devil takes place on earth (though Vat. 4776 has it in Hell). The Flaxman captures some of Dante's sardonic tone when the devil tells Guido "Perhaps you hadn't heard that I was a logician". The Dargent, probably influenced by the Flaxman, is even more effective in capturing the wry Dantean tone.

The Cimbalo wittily renders Guido prostrate before Minos (cf. the renderings of Minos in plates to Canto 5), as does the Sassu.

None of the illustrations, however, find ways to capture Dante's admiration for Ulysses (with whom he fervently longs to speak) or for Guido (who hates dishonor, being one of the few sinners who does not want to be spoken of back on earth (viz; ll. 57–63, used by T. S. Eliot as an epigraph to his "Prufrock"). The Vat. 4776's Guido, however, has some of the poignancy and subtlety of Dante's delineation.

Vatican, Biblioteca Apostolica, MS lat. 4776 (Florentine, ca. 1390–1400).

Vatican, Biblioteca Apostolica, MS lat. 4776 (Florentine, ca. 1390–1400).

Sandro Botticelli, ca. 1478, Kupferstichkabinett, Staatliche Museen, Preussischer Kulturbesitz, Berlin.

Bartolomeo Pinelli, 1826, engraving of drawing.

Gustave Doré, 1861, engraving of drawing.

Vatican, Biblioteca Apostolica, MS lat. 4776 (Florentine, ca. 1390–1400).

Vatican, Biblioteca Apostolica, MS lat. 4776 (Florentine, ca. 1390–1400).

Paris, Bibliothèque Nationale, MS. it. 74 (Florentine, Bartolomeo di Fruosino, ca. 1420).

Sandro Botticelli, ca. 1478, Kupferstichkabinett, Staatliche Museen, Preussischer Kulturbesitz, Berlin.

Federico Zuccaro, ca. 1587, Uffizi, Florence.

John Flaxman, 1793, engraving of drawing.

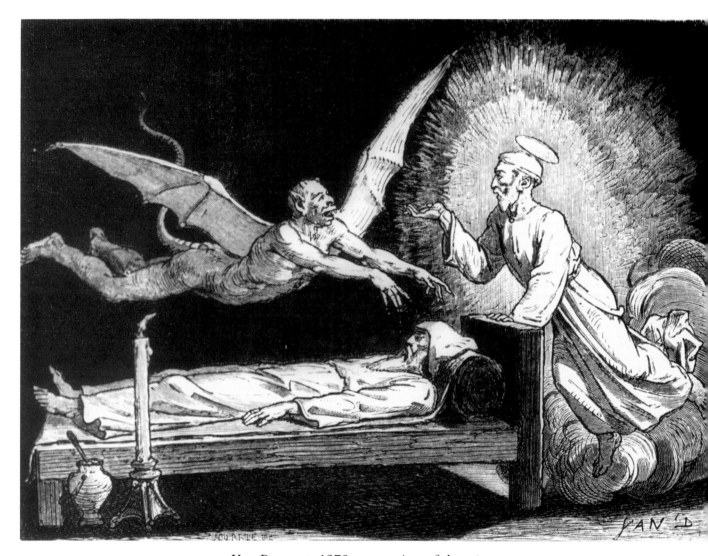

Yan Dargent, 1879, engraving of drawing.

Ebba Holm, 1929, woodcut.

Aligi Sassu, 1987 ed., Milan.

Robert Cimbalo, 1984, mixed media.

28

CANTO VENTESIMOOTTAVO.

1544 ed., Venice, woodcut (from 1564 ed.).

Canto 28

Those who sowed discord on Earth are punished in Hell by various gruesome physical hackings and choppings at the hands of sword-wielding devils. Among the sinners are men that Dante had earlier praised: Mosca Dei Lamberti (who, Dante says in Canto 6, "had set his heart on doing good") and the Provençal poet Bertrand de Born, for whose poetry Dante had expressed his admiration. Thus once again Dante sets up a psychological split in the reader's mind: at least half of our reaction must be compassion.

The Nardo fresco (Spec. Sec.) beautifully maintains this ambivalence of tone: Mosca raises his stumps of arms, Bertrand walks carrying his own severed head, a woman hides her face in her hands, a man winces at the impending stroke of the devil, bodies and parts of bodies lay strewn about. The two miniatures of Vat. 4776 own much to the Nardo, but have their own images as well. In the one, Mohammed leads a parade of sinners who have sown discord in life; Ali, his disciple, is hopping on one foot; in the other, Bertrand is shown speaking to Dante and Virgil as the grim parade continues on to the slashing devil.

Botticelli has, closest to his Dante and Virgil, Piero da Medicina, slit from face to neck, forcing open the mouth of the tribune Curio to show his slit tongue. Bertrand and Mosca are directly behind engaged in a somber exhibition; Mohammed is a few figures to the left. Botticelli clearly takes a whimsical pleasure in creating forms of hacked anatomy beyond Dante's descriptions. One does not, however, sense much emotional involvement on Botticelli's part.

The two Blake illustrations have a curiously handsome devil (one is tempted to call him angel), much in contrast to Dante's description. At the same time, the sinners are shown with great compassion, Mohammed and Ali in the foreground, Bertrand on the far hill in the one, Mosca and Bertrand in the foreground of the other. The expressions on the Dante and Virgil show both compassion and fear. All of the complex, ambivalent reactions of Blake to Dante's work and ideas seem to come into play in these two drawings.

The Doré is perhaps too graphic in the depiction of the shredded, mutilated bodies, and the Bertrand head has a surprisingly harsh expression for the great poet who so influenced Dante.

The Lebrun is one of several the artist did for Canto 28; the reasons for Lebrun's special interest in the imagery of hacked bodies would need a special study. These mute, slashed anatomies may owe something to the Nardo fresco. It is almost totally compassion that invests the two figures. Lebrun is here focusing more on the tragic human condition than any moral lessons Dante the wayfarer might be learning in Hell.

311

Vatican, Biblioteca Apostolica, MS lat. 4776 (Florentine, ca. 1390–1400).

Vatican, Biblioteca Apostolica, MS lat. 4776 (Florentine, ca. 1390–1400).

312

Sandro Botticelli, ca. 1478, Kupferstichkabinett, Staatliche Museen, Preussischer Kulturbesitz, Berlin.

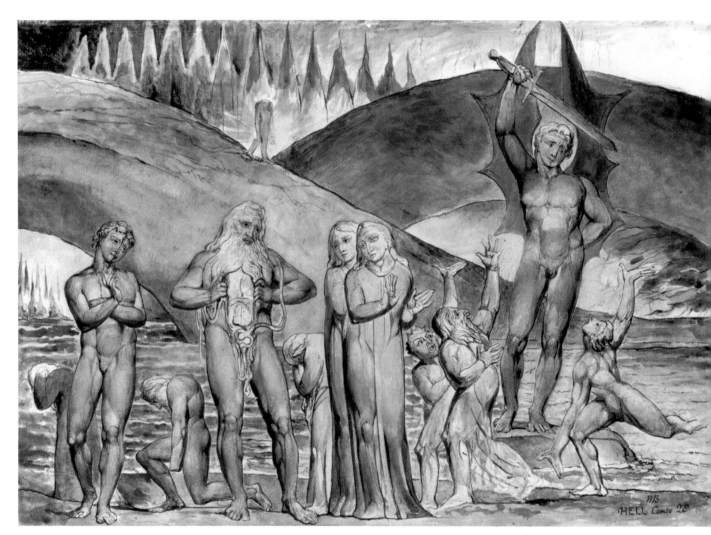

William Blake, 1825–27, watercolor, National Gallery of Victoria.

314

*William Blake, 1825–27, watercolor, National Gallery of
Victoria.*

Gustave Doré, 1861, engraving of drawing.

316

Rico Lebrun, 1962 ed., Northampton, Mass.

29

CANTO VENTESIMONONO.

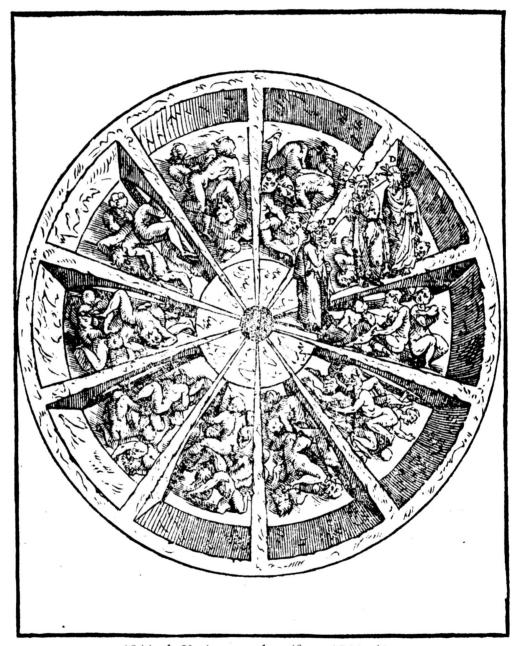

1544 ed., Venice, woodcut (from 1564 ed.).

30

CANTO TRENTESIMO.

1544 ed. Venice, woodcut (from 1564 ed.)

Cantos 29–30

Cantos 29 and 30 complete the ten *bolge* wherein the various categories of simple fraud (according to Aristotle and the Church) are punished. The two Cantos include various sorts of confidence men and women: Alchemists, Impersonators, Forgers, and Liars; the punishments meted out are likewise of the nature of catch-all, forms of disease (leprosy, scabies), dropsy, fever, and madness, save that all are alike in making socializing impossible. Each sinner is condemned to be insufferably close to his neighbor, yet alone (hauntingly conveyed by the Cimbalo); they have denied "the bond of love which all men have from Nature" (ll. 55–57). Their noxiousness is eternally obvious in Hell, as it was hidden on earth.

The Nardo fresco has a magnificent rendering of Griffolino d'Arezzo and Capocchio sitting and scratching themselves side by side, though not looking at one another; they are side by side in the very effective loathsome pit of the Angelica MS, back to back in the Modena miniature, at the bottom left corner of the Vat. 4776, the lower right corners of the Botticelli and the Blake, and they are the main focus of the Mirko and the Lebrun drawings.

The Botticelli has Dante's cousin, Geri del Bello, in the *bolgia* of the Sowers of Discord (just below Bertrand de Born) pointing his finger at Dante for not avenging his murder. The dropsical Maestro Adamo, big-bellied at the center of the drawing, is standing rather than eternally sitting as in Dante (he is similarly standing in the Nardo fresco), and any of the figures biting others could represent the rampaging Gianni Schicchi. Maestro Adamo, Sinon, and Potiphar's wife, deceivers all, are rendered in the lower left corner of the Blake, though hardly with the sardonic wit with which Dante presents them. Maestro Adamo is standing in the Vat. 4776, copying the Nardo; the mad Gianni Schicchi is seen attacking Capocchio in both the Nardo and the Vat. 4776. Fruosino's grotesque and sardonic rendering, rather typical of the artist, is quite appropriate for this canto and its comic vulgarity (Virgil, in fact, berates Dante for his fascination with the vulgar argument of Maestro Adamo and Sinon). Flaxman does not manage this sardonic tone, his Schicchi and Capocchio seem more like Grecian wrestlers. The Marko and the Migneco, however, are right on target tonally.

Nardo di Cione, fresco, Hell, *Florence, S. Maria Novella,*
Strozzi Chapel, ca. 1350s.

Rome, Biblioteca Angelica, MS 1102 (Bolognese, early fifteenth century).

322

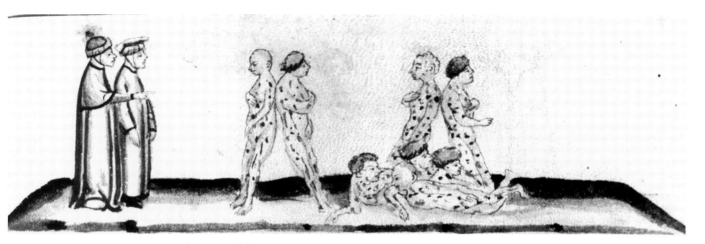

Modena, Biblioteca Estense, MS R.4.8 (Emilian, early fif-teenth century)

Sandro Botticelli, ca. 1478, Kupferstichkabinett, Staatliche Museen, Preussischer Kulturbesitz, Berlin.

William Blake, 1825–27, watercolor, Tate Gallery.

Mirko, 1959 ed. Rome.

Rico Lebrun, 1962, ed., Northampton, Mass.

Robert Cimbalo, 1984, mixed media.

Vatican, Biblioteca Apostolica, MS lat. 4776 (Florentine, ca. 1390-1400).

Paris, Bibliotheque Nationale, MS. it. 74 (Florentine, Bartolomeo di Fruosino, ca. 1420).

328

John Flaxman, 1793, engraving of drawing.

Luigi Marko, 1959, ed., Rome.

Giuseppe Migneco, 1959 ed., Rome.

31

CANTO TRENTESIMOPRIMO.

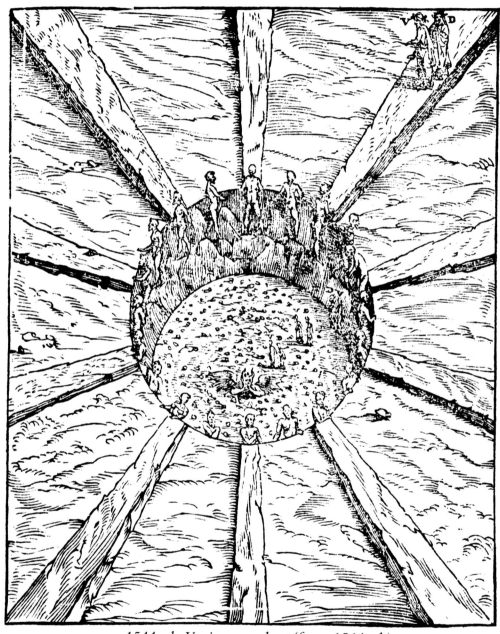

1544 ed., Venice, woodcut (from 1564 ed.)

Canto 31

The Earth-Giants who guard the great circular precipice leading to the three subdivisions of the last circle of Hell are described as without Love or Law, all brute, evil Will: Nimrod of Babylon, with his hunter's horn, Ephialtes and Briareus, Titans who revolted against Jove (chained to contain their explosive violence), Antaeus, unchained and tallest of all. Illustrators have rarely caught, or chosen not to catch, the savage brutality of these giants. Some sort of mystery and fascination seems to loom over these grim creatures at the depths of Hell.

Nardo has, at the bottom of his fresco, three giants at the front of the great well, two at the back. Center-front is Nimrod with his horn, bald and angry; on each side are the Titans Ephialtes and Briareus, bearded and equipped with clubs, shields, and head gear, exuberant, and not really very Dantesque. The Egerton MS epicts Nimrod and Ephialtes, both sufficiently thuggish; the Additional MS depicts the two chained Titans and Antaeus, all rather grandfatherish. The Lombard MS has Ephialtes and Antaeus depicted much like the Additional, though the mysteriousness of the dark pit adds to the total effect.

In the Botticelli, Nimrod at his horn and Antaeus conveying Dante and Virgil to Satan's final pit are at the far side of the precipice, the four chained Titans are Ephialtes, Briareus, Tityos, and Typhon. Dante and Virgil appear five times in the drawing. Virgil embraces the terrified Dante in the upper right quadrant and continues to hold him as they are carried down by Antaeus, just as Dante describes. The drawing as drawing is magnificent and celebrated, but as noted in the Introduction, the semifierceness of the Giants' expressions does not really convey much of the Dantean horror.

Neither does the Zuccaro, where the two Titans in the center (in a well just large enough for the two) suffer enough, but seem more clumsy than fierce, and Antaeus, at the right with Dante and Virgil on his shoulders, seems rather more St. Christopherish than otherwise. The Flaxman, as has been noted in the Introduction, has Antaeus appearing more protective than dangerous. Blake's Giants are almost entirely of a suffering nature (the chained middle figure is kneeling rather than standing as Dante has it). Professor Roe sees them as representative of three of Blake's Four Zoas, suffering the limitations of their own perceptions. The solitary Antaeus of Blake has a face a bit more brutal than the previous Titans, but still quite handsome.

Doré's Antaeus is much like Blake's in power and size (his expression more impassive) and the landscapes of Hell are in both appropriately vast, grand, and fearsome, as the circles of ice approach the Diabolic Will. Scaramuzza's Antaeus is at least as effective as Doré's, though his small central pit does not convey Dante so well. The Manfredini, as is usual for him, manages to catch the awesomeness of this last descent into the central pit of Darkness.

333

London, British Museum, Egerton MS 943 (Emilian or Paduan, second quarter of fourteenth century).

Nardo di Cione, fresco, Hell, *Florence, S. Maria Novella,*
Strozzi Chapel, ca. 1350s.

Quiui era men che notte e men che giorno.
si chel uiso marcaua inanzi poco.
ma io senti sonare un alto corno.

*London, British Museum, Additional MS 19587 (Neapoli-
tan, ca. 1370).*

*Paris, Bibliothèque Nationale, MS it. 2017 (Lombard, ca.
1440).*

336

Sandro Botticelli, ca. 1478, Kupferstichkabinett, Staatliche Museen, Preussischer Kulturbesitz, Berlin.

Federico Zuccaro, ca. 1587, Uffizi, Florence.

John Flaxman, 1793, engraving of drawing.

339

William Blake, 1825–27, watercolor, National Gallery of Victoria.

William Blake, 1825–27, watercolor, National Gallery of Victoria.

Gustave Doré, 1861, engraving of drawing.

Francesco Scaramuzza, 1865, pen drawing.

Manfredo Manfredini, 1907, engraving of drawing.

32

1544 ed., Venice, woodcut (from 1564 ed.).

Canto 32

As Dante and Virgil step onto the ice of the ninth circle of Hell, wherein the Traitorous are locked in the frozen river Cocytus at various depths, a comedic tone similar to the burlesqueness of Cantos 21–22 of the Grafters and 29–30 of the Falsifiers returns to Dante's text. Why this is so, and why this sort of comedy should be mixed with the terrible pathos of the fate of Ugolino and his sons here at the place of ultimate Evil, are questions that have to do at least as much with Dante's artistry as with his theology.

The Vatican 4776 illustration does not convey the illusion of ice particularly well. Dante is shown pulling the hair of Bocca degli Abati, and behind, at the upper right corner, Ugolino gnaws at the head of Archbishop Ruggieri. The splendid Lombard initial has likewise the Bocca and the Ugolino incidents; the hair of each malefactor is frozen into wiry shapes. The Yates-Thompson adds at the left the interview with the brothers Alberti, who are frozen together. The pain of those frozen horizontally is well depicted.

In the Botticelli the Alberti brothers are shown immediately beneath the feet of Dante and Virgil, center right. The feet of the Earth Giants are shown at the top of the drawing, and Dante is shown first looking up at the Giants and then down at the Alberti. The scene with Bocca is just below in the next division, and then below that, at center bottom, the Ugolino-Ruggieri. One has little sense of ice, though many of the sinners are beautifully foreshortened, as we look down from above.

Fuseli's drawing has the feet of the Giants at the back, Dante accidentally kicking the head of Bocca, and Buoso da Duera ready to betray Bocca's identity immediately beneath. The heads of the Traitors, including those of the Alberti brothers, who are butting one another, are drawn with the energy and whimsy for which Fuseli is known. In comparison, the Flaxman heads are blandly done, the clenched teeth in each representing their eternal cold. Blake (who was close to both Fuseli and Flaxman) has a moving and convincing series of prone figures lying in the ice to the left of Bocca, some with crown and scepter. Those frozen in the outcropping of ice at the upper right, the Urizen figure, the upside-down crucified figure, and the others (associated with Blake's Four Zoas by Roe) are certainly not illustrative of Dante's descriptions, though effective in their own right. In the second Blake, Bocca's expression is apropos, but Buoso's hardly so; perhaps Blake's expressed dislike for what he considered Dante's crudity in pulling Bocca's hair is thus shown. In the outcropping to the left, Ugolino at Archbishop Ruggieri's neck (with the clerical hat and crozier prominently displayed) is graphically depicted.

Doré is perhaps the most successful of the illustrators in conveying the ice formations incasing the Traitors, though the outcroppings of the first plate, as with the Blake, involve poetic license effectively used. The Ugolino, not engraved by Pisan as the two previous were, is not so effective in this regard.

Scaramuzza's Bocca (with Buoso in the lower right corner) evokes more pity than Dante's scene, with its vulgar, abusive wit. This missing tonality is supplied in abundance by the Guttuso, where Ugolino, who was starved along with his children in the Tower of Famine, is pictured as emaciated, consumed by hate and vengeance, and quite unheroic.

Vatican, Biblioteca Apostolica, MS lat. 4776 (Florentine, ca. 1390–1400).

Florence, Biblioteca Nazionale, MS B. R. 39 (Lombard, ca. 1400).

London, British Museum, Yates Thompson MS 36 (Priamo della Quercia, mid-fifteenth century).

Sandro Botticelli, ca. 1478, Kupferstichkabinett, Staatliche Museen, Preussischer Kulturbesitz, Berlin.

Henry Fuseli, 1774, Dante and Virgil on the Ice of Cocytus, *pen and wash, British Museum.*

John Flaxman, 1793, engraving of drawing.

William Blake, 1825–27, watercolor, Fogg Gallery.

351

William Blake, 1825–27, watercolor, Birmingham Art Gallery.

Gustave Doré, 1861, engraving of drawing

353

Gustave Doré, 1861, engraving of drawing.

354

Gustave Doré, 1861, engraving of drawing.

355

Francesco Scaramuzza, 1865, pen drawing.

Renato Guttuso, 1969, Rome.

33

CANTO TRENTESIMOTERZO.

1544 ed., Venice, woodcut (from 1564 ed.).

Canto 33

Ugolino's pathetic, terrible story of his final days on earth has inspired artists from Joshua Reynolds's canvas of 1773 to the present day. The paintings and sculptures are matched in their profusion only by the similarly pathetic scene of Paolo and Francesca. The scene of Ugolino and his sons dying in the Tower, however, takes place on earth (as with the seduction scene of Francesca), not in Hell, and so is not really appropriate to this volume. One would need, in any case, a volume like the Locella (see Bibliography) to do justice to the Ugolino theme in art. I do, however, include the renditions of Fuseli (1806), Delacroix (1860), Rodin (1882), and Aldo Greco (1974), as well as (to select the best) the illustrations in the editions of 1804 (Sabatelli), 1817 (Ademolli), 1861 (Doré), and 1865 (Scaramuzza).

The illustrations to Canto 33, aside from those in the Tower of Famine, do not add much to those of Canto 32. The Vatican 4776 illustration is largely a repetition of the previous with the mountainous background added. The Botticelli is a more interesting composition than his previous, but he keeps repeating the motif of Traitor biting Traitor, though Dante mentions it only with regard to Ugolino and Ruggieri. (It is, however, quite appropriate to extend this sort of punishment to others of the Traitors). In the third division of this last circle are those who have been traitorous to guests; they have their eyes permanently frozen over with ice. Botticelli has many moving vignettes of the prone sinners so afflicted. Dante and Virgil converse with Frate Alberigo, though Botticelli is unable to convey the grim humor of the conversation: we hear that Alberigo's body and that of his neighbor, Branca d'Oria, still live and walk the earth, possessed by devils.

The Lombard miniature manages a more convincing sense than the Botticelli of sinners actually lying beneath real ice, though Ugolino and Ruggieri seem to be wholly above the surface, contrary to Dante's text. In the Stradanus, they are submerged in a pit, while their compatriots are locked in ice. Ugolino's earthly fate in the tower with his children is depicted in the upper half of the plate.

Blake's Ugolino is once again reminiscent of Blake's misguided, suffering Urizen, while his Archbishop Ruggieri again emphasizes Blake's anti-clericalism, with the large clerical hat above the ice and the great crozier at the base of the drawing. Cimbalo's drawing renders the literal horror of the scene, without empathy for either man.

Manfredini's fantastic ice forms are most likely influenced by Doré's, and actually illustrate Canto 34, ll. 10–12:

> I stood now where the souls of the last class
> (with fear my verses tell it) were covered wholly;
> they shone below the ice like straws in glass.

Vatican, Biblioteca Apostolica, MS lat. 4776 (Florentine, ca. 1390–1400).

Paris, Bibliothèque Nationale, MS it. 2017 (Lombard, ca. 1440).

360

*Sandro Botticelli, ca. 1478, Kupferstichkabinett,
Staatliche Museen, Preussischer Kulturbesitz, Berlin.*

Stradanus (Jan van der Straet), 1587, Laurentian Library,
Florence.

Luigi Sabatelli, 1804 ed.

Henry Fuseli, 1806, Ugolino and His Sons in the Tower of Famine, *engraving after oil painting, Kunsthaus, Zurich.*

Luigi Ademolli, 1817, engraving of drawing.

365

William Blake 1825–27, watercolor, Fogg Gallery.

Eugene Delacroix, 1860, Ugolino and His Sons, *oil, Ordrupgaard Collection, Copenhagen.*

Gustave Doré, 1861, engraving of drawing.

Francesco Scaramuzza, 1865, pen drawing.

Auguste Rodin, 1882, Ugolino and His Sons, *Paris, Musée Rodin.*

Manfredo Manfredini, 1907, engraving of drawing.

Aldo Greco, 1974 ed., Ravenna.

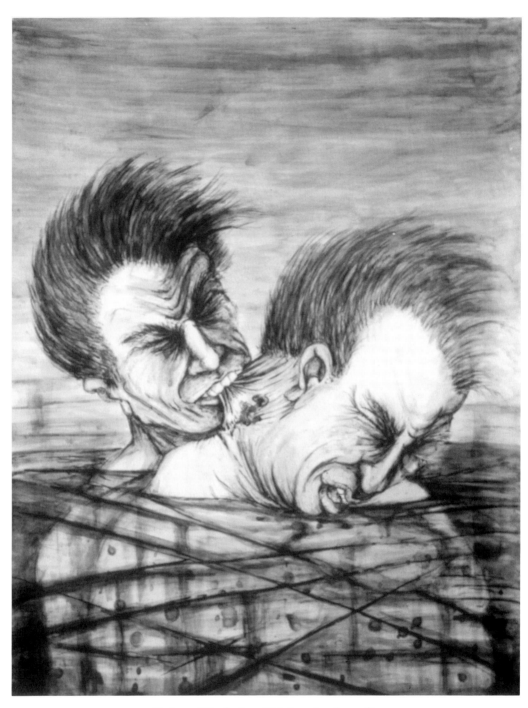

Robert Cimbalo, 1984, mixed media.

34

CANTO TRENTESIMOQVARTO.

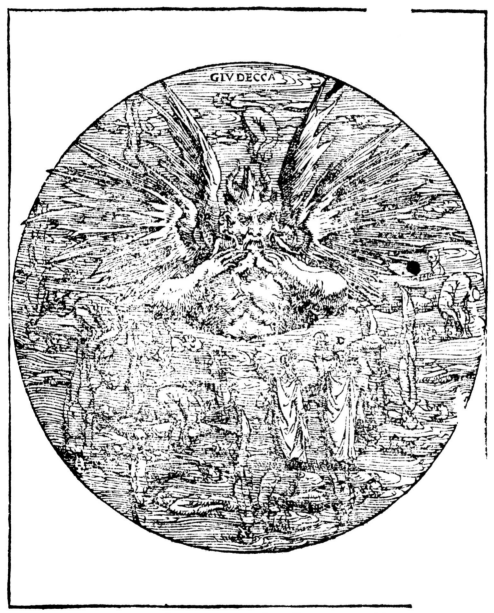

1544 ed., Venice, woodcut (from 1564 ed.)

Canto 34

The originality of Dante's Satan lies not so much in his three-facedness as a perversion of the Trinity (earlier "Last Judgments," such as the mosaic in the Baptistery in Florence, had three-faced Satans), but in his immobility, his being locked in ice at the center of the earth, and in his eternal tears, cut off from all light, warmth, and Love. Yet even here Brutus accepts his fate with dignity, writhing without a word. Dante's ambivalence concerning evil and punishment thus extends even to the final reaches of darkness.

Traditional frescos of three-faced Satans often had two of the faces as beasts, dragonish or wolfish (*cf.* in the Special Section those in the Baptistery, the Camposanto, the Arena Chapel, and Santa Maria Novella), often, too, with a face at the abdomen, groin, or tip of a tail (*cf.* in the Spec. Sec., the Giotto, Traini, Modena, Bartolo). The two side heads of the Vatican 4776 miniature are animal rather than human heads. Satan bears a club in one hand and a serpent in the other (all after **Nardo**). Dante is depicted as having fallen with fear ("lost life's breath") on the ice of Judecca. The expression on Brutus's face has some of the dignity described by Dante. In the second Vat. 4776 plate, it is presumably Dante or Virgil in robes climbing from the shoulder of Satan down to the center of Hell, (and then up to the other side of the world). In the third Vat. 4776 plate, Dante and Virgil emerge to the starlight of the southern hemisphere and Mount Purgatory.

The illumination in the Florentine MS in the Morgan Library in New York City has a Satan with three separate heads rather than the usual head with three faces. The six wings and the hairy body are well depicted; the imbecilic expressions of Satan and the *simpliciter* rendering of the falling sinners and of the descending Dante and Virgil are not so effective, though the whole design has power. The Stradanus is a similar design, with much greater sophistication and sense of scale.

The Vatican 365 and the 1544 woodcut edition both render two similar episodes: Satan first top half, followed by Satan's legs extending into a valley on the other side of the world. Vatican 365's hairless Satan is more human-like than 1544's; his wings are curiously oval. Dante and Virgil emerge into a beautiful valley consistent with the lovely landscapes throughout Vatican 365's renditions of Hell, though here more appropriate than usual. The 1544 edition has effective illustrations of Satan locked with the sinners in the ice "like straws in glass," and then of a rocky southern valley surrounded by ocean and, further on, Mount Purgatory. The little woodcut vignette from Giolito's 1555 edition has more charm than interpretive power.

Botticelli's hairy Satan has three magnificently ferocious faces, though one misses the tears Dante describes. Brutus's face is without significant character. In the full-length drawing, Satan's genitals are at the center of the earth. The Dante and Virgil figures are seen first at the upper right, with Dante fearing the sight of Satan, then Dante holding on to Virgil as he climbs downwards, turning at the center of the earth to an upward climb, and finally, at the lower right, looking upwards at the stars from a stony pit or valley.

Flaxman's drawing is largely design and nonserious, though he does include the tears of Satan. Doré's, without the tears, is meant much more seriously. Doré's scale is vast and effective, and Satan locked in ice conveys both anger and despair in a tomb of eternal cold and darkness. Dargent's drawing, clearly derived from Doré, has a weeping Satan, but one too human, more a hairless, sad freak than a monstrous, devouring Giant. The Scaramuzza focuses on the climb downward on the monster's hairy body and is a charming fantasy, appropriate for the leaving behind of the somber experiences of the *Inferno*.

*New York, the Pierpont Morgan Library, MS 676 (Italian,
late fourteenth century).*

375

Vatican, Biblioteca Apostolica, MS lat 4776 (Florentine, ca. 1390–1400).

Vatican, Biblioteca Apostolica, MS lat. 4776 (Florentine, ca. 1390–1400).

Vatican, Biblioteca Apostolica, MS lat. 4776 (Florentine, ca. 1390–1400).

Vatican, Biblioteca Apostolica, MS Urb. lat. 365 (Guglielmo Giraldi & assistants, ca. 1478).

377

*Vatican, Biblioteca Apostolica, MS Urb. lat. 365
(Guglielmo Giraldi & assistants, ca. 1478).*

*Sandro Botticelli, ca. 1478, Kupferstichkabinett,
Staatliche Museen, Preussischer Kulturbesitz, Berlin.*

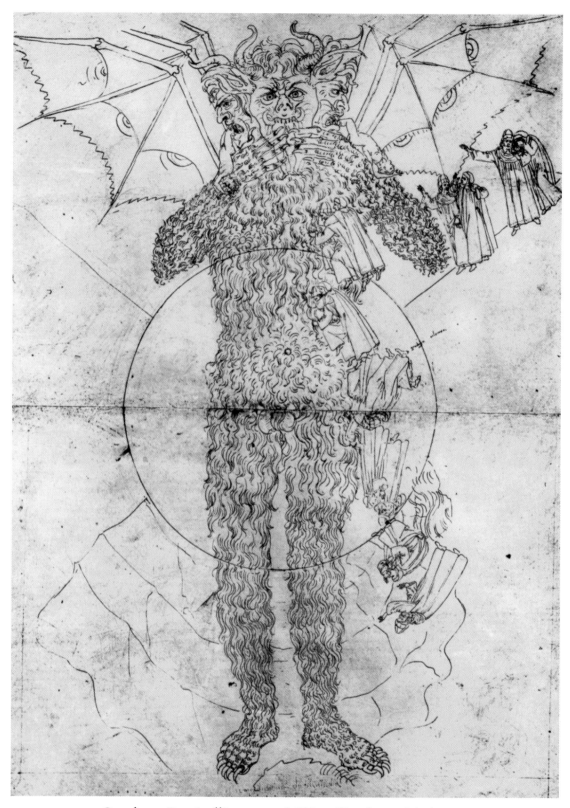

*Sandro Botticelli, ca. 1478, Kupferstichkabinett,
Staatliche Museen, Preussischer Kulturbesitz, Berlin.*

1544 ed., Venice, woodcut (from 1564 ed.).

1555 ed., Venice, woodcut.

382

Stradanus (Jan van der Straet) 1587, Laurentian Library, Florence.

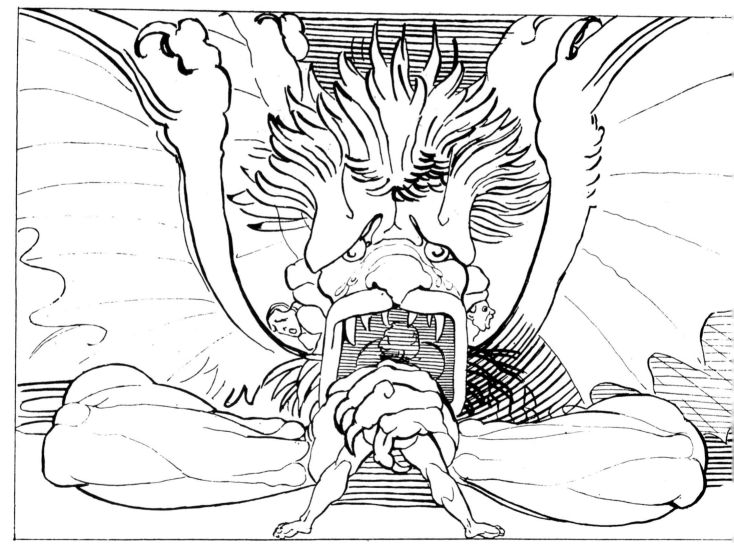

John Flaxman, 1793, engraving of drawing.

Gustave Doré, 1861, engraving of drawing.

Francesco Scaramuzza, 1865, pen drawing.

386

Yan Dargent, 1879, engraving of drawing.

Select List of Illustrated Editions

THE FOLLOWING LIST EXCLUDES MANY EDITIONS THAT HAVE ILLUSTRATIONS OF NO REAL SIGNIFI-cance or of portraits of Dante or diagrams of Hell only. The *Catalogue of the Dante Collection* of the Cornell University Library (1898–1900, 1920), and the actual Cornell University Library catalog listing of editions thereafter is the basic source for this listing, supplemented by the *National Union Catalog* and its supplements, *Volkmann's* list, the *Mambelli* bibliography, and the *Enciclopedia Dantesca*.

1481	Florence, Nicholo di Lorenzo della Magna (nineteen copper-plate engravings after Botticelli)
1487	Brescia, Boninus de Boninis (sixty-eight woodcuts)
1491	March. Venice, Bernardino Benali and Matthio da Parma (100 woodcuts)
1491	November. Venice, Pietro Cremonese. (100 woodcuts)
1506	Florence, Filippo di Giunta (*Inf.* I only)
1512	Venice, Bernardino Stagnino (100 woodcuts)
1544	Venice, Francesco Marcolini (eighty-seven woodcuts)
1555	Venice, Gabriel Giolito e fratelli (initials)
1564	Venice, G. Marchio Sessa e fratelli (rep. 1544 ed. woodcuts)
1588	Florence, Drawings by F. Zuccaro (in Uffizi)
1588	Florence, Drawings by G. Stradanus (in Biblioteca Laurenziana)
1757–58	Venice, Antonio Zatta (106 copper engravings, several hands)
1778	London and Leghorn, G. T. Masi & Co. (*Inf.* 33 only)
1784	Venice, Zatta e figli (reduced reprints of 1757–58 ed.)
1793	Rome, Tommaso Piroli (ill. Flaxman)
1804–9	Pisa, Società letteraria (*Inf.* 33, ill. L. Sabatelli)
1813	Paris, Salmon (ill. Sofia Giacomelli)
1817–19	Florence, All' Insegna dell' Ancora (ill. Ademolli)
1819–21	Bologna, Gamberini & Parmeggiani (ill. Macchiavelli)
1828	Florence, Passigli Borghi & Co. (*Inf.* 5 only)
1830	Florence, Tipografia all' insegna di Dante (*Inf.* 5 & 14 only)

1840–41 Florence, David Passigli (*Inf.* 5 only)
1840–42 Florence, Fabris (ill. D. Fabris)
1841   Pforzheim, Finck & Co., (*Inf.* 33 only)
1846–48 Florence, Tip del Vulcano (ill. V. Guzzini)
1849   Munich, A. Durr (ill. B. Genelli)
1854   London, Chapman & Hall (ill. G. Scharf)
1854   Paris, Bry ainé (ill. Etex)
1858–65 London, Boone (Lord Vernon ed.)
1859   Paris, Delarue (ill. A. Sturler)
1861   Paris, Hachette & Cie (ill. Doré)
1864   Milan, G. Schiepatti (ill. S. Mazza)
1864   Milan, Daelli & Co. (March 1491 repro.)
1865   Florence, G. Polverini (ill. various hands)
1865–75 Parma, C. Saccani (ill. Scaramuzza)
1865   Milan, F. Pagoni (ill. C. Barbieri, F. Maurizio, F. Faruffini)
1868   Naples, Rondinella (ill. R. Andreoli)
1879   Paris, Garnier (ill. Y. Dargent)
1892   London, T. F. Unwin (ill. Stradanus, see Biblio. Symonds)
1896   London, Lawrence and Bullen (ill. Botticelli, see Biblio. Lippmann)
1902   Florence, Alinari (various hands, 2nd ed. 1922)
1904   Valdagno, Giovanni Galla (ill. J. A. Koch, see Biblio. Valle)
1906   Berlin, G. Grote'sche (ill. Franz Stassen)
1907   Florence, Nerbini (ill. M. Manfredini & T. Scarpelli)
1907   Milan, P. Carrare (ill. N. Sanesi)
1908   Milan, Fratelli Treves (ill. Zuccaro et. al.; see Biblio. Ricci)
1912   Terni, Alterocca (*Galleria Dantesca*, various artists)
1912   Paris, H. Laurens (ill. F. M. Roganeau).
1918   Florence, Sansoni (various artists)
1919   Zagreb, Nakl Grafickoga (ill. Mirka Rackoga).
1921   Zurich, Amalthea Verlag (ill. Franz von Bayros).
1924   Turin, Unione Typografico (various artists).
1925   Berlin, (*Dante Block Buch*, ill. Klaus Wrage).
1928   Paris, Renourd (ill. Gio Colucci).
1928   Milan, Casa Ed. di Dante (ill. Amos Nattini).
1929   Copenhagen, G. Gads Forlag (ill. Ebba Holm).
1930   Paris, J. Schiffren (ill. Edy Legrand).
1933   London, Oxford University Press (ill. J. D. Batten).
1943   Novara, I. G. de Agostini (ill. G. B. Galizzi).
1944   New York, Modern Library (ill. George Groz).
1946   Garden City, Doubleday (ill. Umberto Romano).
1950   Paris, J. Porson (ill. Edouard Georg).
1953   Princeton, N.J., Princeton Univ. Press (ill. W. Blake, see Biblio. Roe).
1954   Stuttgart, Dr. Riederer (ill. V. Orasch).
1956   Turin, S.A.I.E. (ill. Emma Mazza)
1957   Eutin am Kellersee, Handabzugholmpress K. Wrage (ill. Klaus Wrage, *Dante Blochbuch*, see above, 1925).
1959   Buenos Aires, Libreria "El Ateneo" (ill. B. Kriukov).
1959   Rome, DeLuca (various artists, see Biblio. *Omaggio a Dante*).
1960   Paris, Editions d'art Les Heures Claires (ill. S. Dali).
1961   Moscow, Gos. izd-vo khudozh (ill. M. Pikov).

1963	Northampton, Mass., Kanthos Press (ill. Rico Lebrun).
1964	Bari, Laterza (ill. Tono Zancanaro).
1964	Florence, La Nuova Italia Editrice (ill. Anthony DeWitt).
1964	Rome, Armando Curcio (ill. Domenico Purificato).
1964	New York, Abrams (ill. Robert Rauschenberg).
1965	Madrid, Biblioteca Nueva (ill. V. Turcios).
1965	Bergisch Gladbach, Lubbe Verlag (ill. Karl Kunz).
1965	Lugano, Guilio Topi (ill. Mario Marioni).
1968	New York, Washington Square Press (ill. Harry Bennett)
1969	Princeton, N. J., Princeton Univ. Press (illuminations, see Biblio., Brieger).
1969	New York, Grossman Publishers (ill. Leonard Baskin).
1969	Rome, Galleria d'Arte il Gabbiano (ill. Renato Guttuso).
1971	Bloomington, Indiana Univ. Press (ill. R. M. Powers).
1974	Ravenna, Centro Dantesca (sculpture of Aldo Greco)
1975	Ravenna, Centro Dantesca (contemporary sculpture).
1978	Ravenna, Centro Dantesca (fifty Italian artists, see Biblio. *Cinquanta*).
1980	Berkeley, Univ. of California Press (ill. Barry Moser).
1983	London, Talfourd Press (ill. Tom Phillips).
1985	Florence, Pierluigi Bigazzi (ill. Quinto Martini).
1987	Milan, Mazzotta (ill. Aligi Sassu).

Select Bibliography

T HIS BIBLIOGRAPHY LISTS THOSE WORKS ACTUALLY CONSULTED. IT IS NOT IN ANY WAY A GUIDE to general literary criticism of the *Inferno*, but to the specific literature on illustration of the *Inferno*. My own bibliographic search has been conducted through the Cornell University *Catalogue to the Dante Collection* (1898–1900, 1920) and the University Library catalog, together with the Colomb de Batines and Ferrazzi, the *National Union Catalog* and its supplements, and the annual bibliographies of *Dante Studies*, the *Modern Language Association* (MLA) and *Studi Danteschi*. Many of the books listed below contain very useful bibliographies to special areas, i.e., the Branca, Brieger, Donati, *Enciclopedia Dantesca*, Fallani, Kraus, Mambelli, Toynbee, Ulivi, and Volkmann.

Apollonio, Mario. "Immagini Dantesche nelle arti." In *Temi Dantesche ad Orvieto*. Milan: Arti Grafiche Ricordi, 1965.

Auerbach, Erich. "Farinata and Cavalcante." In his *Mimesis: The Representation of Reality in Western Literature*. Princeton, N.J.: Princeton University Press, 1953.

Auvray, Lucien. "Les miniatures du manuscrit de l'enfer à Chantilly." In *Dante: Mélanges de critique et d'érudition française publiés à l'occasion du VIe centenaire de la mort du poète*. Paris: Societé d'Études Italiennes, 1921.

Bassermann, Alfred. *Dante's Spuren in Italien*. Heidelberg: C. Winter, 1897.

Benedite, Leonce. "Dante et Rodin." In *Dante: Mélanges* . . . (*see* Auvray)

Berenson, Bernard. "Dante's Visual Images, and His Early Illustrators." In *Nation* 58 (1 February 1894):82–83.

———. "Botticelli's Illustrations to the Divina Commedia" *Nation* 63 (12 November 1896): 363–64.

Bertolini, Lica. *Camposanto monumentale di Pisa: affreschi e sinopie*. Pisa: Opera della Primaziale Pisana, 1960.

Besso, Marco. *La fortuna di Dante fuori d'Italia*. Florence: Olschki, 1912.

Biagi, Guido. *Illustrazioni della Divina Commedia dell'artista fiammingo Giovanni Stradano (1587)*. Florence: Alinari, 1893. (English ed., with an introduction by J. Addington Symonds, London: T. F. Unwin, 1892.)

————. *La Divina Commedia nella figurazione artistica e nel secolare commento.* 3 vol. Turin: Unione Tipografico, 1921, 1934, 1939.

Blake, William. *See* Klonsky; Roe.

Boehn, Max Von. "Dante Illustration." In *Divina Commedia,* edited by Karl Witte. Berlin: Askanischer Verlag, 1923.

Bosco, Umberto, ed. *Enciclopedia Dantesca,* 6 vols. Rome: Istituto della Enciclopedia Italiana, 1970–76.

Botticelli, Sandro. *See* Clark, Lippmann.

Branca, Vittore and Ettore Caccia eds. *Dante nel mondo.* Florence: Olschki, 1965.

Brieger, Peter, ed. *Illuminated Manuscripts of the Divine Comedy.* 2 vol. Princeton, N.J.: Bollingen Foundation, 1969.

Caccia, Ettore. *See* Branca.

Cassell, Anthony. *Dante's Fearful Art of Justice.* Toronto: University of Toronto Press, 1985.

Catalogo della rassegna di scultura dantesca contemporanea. Ravenna: Centro Dantesca, 1975.

Catalogue of the Dante Collection. Cornell University Library, Ithaca, N.Y.: 1898–1900, 1920. *See* Koch, Fowler.

Chan, Victor. "Transformations of a Dantesque Image." *Arts Magazine* 55 : 7 (March 1981):80–84.

Cinquanta artisti Italiani illustrano la Divine Commedia. Catalog, Ravenna: Centro Dantesca, 1978.

Clark, Kenneth. *The Drawings of Sandro Botticelli for Dante's Divine Comedy.* New York: Harper and Row, 1976.

Colomb de Batines, Paul. *Bibliografia Dantesca.* Prato, Italy: Tip. Aldina Editrice, 1845–46.

D'Ancona, M. L. "Bartolomeo di Fruosino." *Art Bulletin.* 43 (1961):81–97.

————. *Miniatura e miniatori a Firenze dal XIV al XVI secolo.* Florence, Olschki, 1962.

D'Ancona, Paolo. *La Divina Commedia e le arti figurative.* Bergamo: Instituto Italiano D'Arte Grafiche, 1948.

Dante Studies, with the Annual Report of the Dante Society. Cambridge, Mass.: 1882–

Il Dante Urbinate della Biblioteca Vaticana (Codex Urb. Lat. 365), Vatican City, 1965.

Dante Virgil Geryon, Catalog, Staatsgalerie, Stuttgart, 1980.

DeSanctis, Francesco, ed. *La Divina Commedia illustrata,* Rome: Editione di Cultura, 1961.

Donati, Lamberto. *Il Botticelli e le prime illustrazione della Divina Commedia.* Florence: Olschki, 1962.

Eliot, T. S. "Dante." In *The Sacred Wood.* London: Methuen, 1920.

Elwert, Theodore. "Dantedeutung und Danteillustration." *Deutsches Dante-Jahrbuch* 44–45 1967: 34–58.

Fallani, Giovanni. "Lectura Dantis: degli artisti contemporanei." In his *Dante Moderno.* Ravenna: Longo Editore, 1980.

————. "La Divina Commedia nell'interpretazione dello scultore Omero Piccione." *L'Alighieri,* 25 1984:73–74.

Ferrazzi, Giuseppe, *Manuale Dantesca,* Bassano: Tip. Sante Pozzato, 1865–77.

Fogoliari, Gino. "Gli illustratori della Divina Commedia." In *Dante.* Milan: Fratelli Treves, 1921.

Foligno, Cesare. *Dante.* Bergamo, Instituto Italiano d'Arte Grafiche, 1920.

Fowler, Mary, ed. *Catalogue of the Dante Collection: Additions 1898–1920* Ithaca, N.Y.: Cornell University Library, 1921.

Fucilla, Joseph. "Dante." In *PMLA Annual Bibliography* 1958–.

Gizzi, Corrado, ed. *Sassu e Dante*. Milan: G. Mazzatta, 1987.

Gosebruch, Martin. "Von Wesentlicher Dante-Illustration." in *Dante Alighieri*. Wurzburg: Leo Loenhardt Verlag, 1966.

Gosling, Nigel. *Gustave Doré*. New York: Praeger, 1973.

Greco, Aldo. *See* Perrone, P.

Gronau, Hans. *Andrea Orcagna und Nardo Di Cione*. Berlin: Deutscher Kunstverlag, 1937.

Guttuso, Renato. *disegni danteschi*. Rome: Galleria d'arte il gabbiano, 1969.

———. *Il Dante di Guttuso*. Milan: Mondadori, 1970.

Hughes, Dorothy G. "Trecento Illustrations of the Divina Commedia." *Annual Report of the Dante Society* 77 (1959): 1–40.

Klonsky, Milton. *Blake's Dante*. New York: Harmony Books, 1980.

Koch, Joseph Anton. *See* Valle.

Koch, Theodore Wesley, ed. *Catalogue of the Dante Collection*. Ithaca, N.Y.: Cornell University Library, 1898–1900.

Kraus, Francis Xavier. *Dante*. Berlin: G. Grote'sche Verlagsbuchhandlung, 1897.

———. *Luca Signorelli: Illustrationem zu Dantes D.C.* Freiburg: J. C. B. Mohr, 1892.

Lebrun, Rico. *Drawings for Dante's Inferno by Rico Lebrun*. Northampton, Mass.: The Kanthos Press, 1963.

Lippmann, Friedrich. *Drawings by Sandro Botticelli for Dante's Divina Commedia*. London: Lawrence and Bullen, 1896.

Locella, Guglielmo, *Dante's Francesca Da Rimini in der Literatur, Bildenden Kunst und Musik*. Eszlingen: Paul Neff Verlag, 1913.

Mambelli, Giuliano. *Gli annali delle edizioni Dantesche*. Bologna: Nicola Zanichelli, 1931.

Mariani, Valerio. "Dante e le arti figurative dell'ottocentro." In *Atti del congresso nazionale di studi Danteschi*. Florence: Leo S. Olschki Editore, 1962.

———. *Conversatione d'arte*. Napoli: Libreria Scientifica editrice, 1957.

Meiss, Millard, ed. *Illuminated Manuscripts of the Divine Comedy*. 2 vol. Princeton, N. J.: Princeton University Press, 1969.

Morel, Camille. *Une illustration de l'Enfer de Dante*. Paris: H. Welter, 1896.

Omaggio a Dante degli artisti Italiani d'oggi. Rome: Luigi De Luca, 1959.

Omaggio a Dante Alighieri nel VII centenario della nascita, Bergamo: Gli Amici Dei Sacri Lari, 1965.

Omaggio a Dante. Bologna: Patron, 1966.

Perrone, P. ed. *Aldo Greco*. Ravenna: Centro Dantesco, 1974.

Pinelli, Bartolomeo. *Invenzioni sul poema di Dante Alighieri*. 3 vol. Rome: no publisher listed, 1824–26.

Plunkett, (Count). "One of Dante's Illustrators: Pinelli." *Lectures of the Dante Society*. [London: 1904], 195–210.

Pollard, Alfred W. *Early Illustrated Books*. London: Kegan Paul, Trench, Trubner & Co., 1893.

Pope-Hennessy, J. *A Sienese Codex of the Divine Comedy*. London: Phaidon Press, 1947.

Pound, Ezra. "Dante." In his *The Spirit of Romance*. London: J. M. Dent, 1910.

Ricci, Corrado. *La Divina Commedia illustrada*. Milan: U. Hoepli, 1898.

———. *La Divina Commedia di Dante Alighieri nell'arte del Cinquecentro*. Milan: Fratelli Treves, 1908.

Roe, Albert. *Blake's Illustrations to the Divine Comedy.* Princeton, N. J.: Princeton University Press, 1953.

Rotili, Mario. *I codici Danteschi miniati a Napoli.* Naples: Libreria Scientifica Editore, 1972.

Rotondi, Pasquale. "Gli affreschi della Cappella di San Brizio e L'arte di Luca Signorelli." In *Temi Danteschi ad Orvieto.* Milan: Arti Graphiche Ricordi, 1965.

Salmi, Mario. *Luca Signorelli,* Novara: Instituto Geografico de Agostini, 1953.

———. *Italian Illuminated Manuscripts.* New York: H. N. Abrams, 1954.

Samek-Ludovici, Sergio. *La Divina Commedia con riproduzione di miniature.* Rome: Instituto Poligrafico dello Stato, 1965.

Santayana, George. *Three Philosophic Poets.* Cambridge, Mass.: Harvard University Press, 1910.

Scartazzini, Govanni A. "Scaramuzza's Illustrationen zur Divina Commedia." *Allgemeine Zeitung.* 1876, no. 202.

Schneider, René. "Dante et Delacroix." In *Melanges sur Dante. See* Auvray

Schubring, Paul. *Illustrationen zu Dante's Gottlicher Komodie: Italien, 14 bis 16 Jahrhundert.* Zurich: Amalthea Verlag, 1931.

Seznec, Jean. "Dante and Delacroix." In *The World of Dante,* edited by Cecil Grayson. New York: Oxford University Press, 1980.

Singleton, Charles. *See* Brieger.

Studi Danteschi. Florence, 1920– .

Symonds, J. Addington. "Prefatory Notes." In *Illustrations to the Divine Comedy of Dante. Executed by the Flemish Artist, John Stradanus, 1587,* edited by Guido Biagi. London: T. F. Unwin, 1892.

Symmons, Sarah. "John Flaxman and Francisco Goya: Infernos Transcribed." *Burlington Magazine* 113 (September 1971): 508–12.

———. "Gericault, Flaxman and 'Ugolino'." *Burlington Magazine,* 115 (October 1973) 671–72.

Toesca, Pietro. *Storia dell'arte Italiana.* Turin: Union Tipografico-Editrice Torinese, 1951.

Toynbee, Paget. "The Earliest English Illustrators of Dante." In his *Dante Studies.* New York: Oxford University Press, 1921.

———. "Dante in English Art." In his *Britain's Tribute to Dante,* London: Oxford University Press, p. 1921.

Ulivi, Ferruccio. "Dante e l'interpretazione figurativa." In *Omaggio a Dante,* edited by G. B. Pighi. Bologna: Patron, 1966.

———. "Illustrazioni Dantesche." *Nuova Antologia* 511 (1970): 121–28.

Valle, Emilio, ed. *Iconografia Dantesca del pittore Giuseppe Antonio Koch.* Valdagno: Giovanni Galla, 1904.

Venturi, Adolfo. *Il Botticelli interprete di Dante.* Florence: La Monnier, 1921.

Vernon, Lord [George Warren]. *L'Inferno.* London: G. Boone, 1865.

Volkmann, Ludwig. *Iconografia Dantesca.* (English ed.) London: H. Grevel & Co., 1899.

———. "Neue Beitrage zur Iconographia Dantesca." *Deutsches Dante-Jahrbuch* 8 (1924): 60–98.

Xiaosheng, Xing. "Li Shaowen's Illustrations for Dante's 'Divine Comedy'." *Chinese Literature* (March 1983): 113–16.

Yates, Frances A. "Transformations of Dante's Ugolino." *Journal of the Warburg and Courtauld Institute.* 14 (1951): 91–117.

Yeats, William Butler. "William Blake and his Illustrations to the Divine Comedy." In his *Essays and Introductions*. New York: Macmillan, 1961.

Zingarelli, Nicola, ed. *La Divina Commedia*. Bergamo: Instituto Italiano d'Arti Grafiche-Editore, 1948.

Index

Discussion of the plates and artists is in normal typeface; reference is to page numbers. The plates themselves are indexed in **boldface**; reference is to canto numbers. To avoid redundancy, the notes that introduce the plates for each canto are only lightly indexed here, since generally each plate in the given section is given a brief mention. The abbreviation "S.S." denotes the Special Section's plates (boldface) and notes (normal).

Ademolli, Luigi, 20; **2, 5, 6, 13, 21, 25, 33**
Angelico, Fra, 17, 276; **S.S.**
Aquinas, St. Thomas, 14
Aristotle, 14, 320
Auerbach, Erich, 12, 13, 149

Baptistery (Florence), 17, 276, 374; **S.S.**
Bartolo, Taddeo di (Hell, fresco, Collegiata, San Gimignano), 17, 276, 374; **S.S.**
Baskin, Leonard, 24; **17, 20**
Bassermann, Alfred, 28
Batten, J. D., 23; **2**
Benvenuto da Imola, 17
Berenson, Bernard, 11, 14, 15, 16, 21, 22
Berlin, **8, 11, 17–29, 31–33, 34**
Biblioteca Angelica (Rome), **1, 9–10, 12–13, 15–16**; MS 1102, **21, 29**. *See also* Botticelli
Biblioteca Apostolica Vaticana. *See* Manuscripts—Vatican
Biblioteca Comunale (Imola). *See* Manuscripts—Imola
Biblioteca del Seminario (Padua). *See* Manuscript—Padua
Biblioteca Estense (Modena). *See* Manuscripts—Modena
Biblioteca Girolamini (Naples). *See* Manuscripts—Naples
Biblioteca Laurenziana (Florence). *See* Manuscripts—Florence
Biblioteca Marciana (Venice). *See* Manuscripts—Venice
Biblioteca Nazionale (Florence). *See* Manuscripts—Florence
Biblioteca Riccardiana (Florence). *See* Manuscripts—Florence
Bibliotheque Nationale (Paris). *See* Manuscripts—Paris
Birmingham Art Gallery (England). *See* Blake, William

Blake, William, 12, 15, 19, 21, 31; **1, 3, 4–6, 8, 10, 13, 14, 16, 18–21, 22, 23, 25, 28, 29, 31, 32, 33**
Bologna. *See* Modena, Giovanni da
Botticelli, Sandro, 11, 12, 15, 16, 18, 20, 23, 47, 185; **1, 8–13, 15–29, 31–33, 34**
Breiger, Peter, 11, 14, 15, 18
Brescia. *See Divine Comedy;* editions: 1487
British Museum and Library (London). *See* Manuscripts—London
Budapest. *See* Manuscripts—Budapest
Burne-Jones, Edward, 21

Camposanto, Pisa. *See* Frescos
Chantilly. *See* Manuscripts—Chantilly
Chirico, Giorgio de, 23; **1**
Ciardi, John, 12, 24
Cimbalo, Robert, 25, 87; **1, 5, 7, 27, 29, 33**
Cione, Nardo di (Inferno fresco, Santa Maria Novella, Florence), 17, 18, 57, 77, 87, 107, 118, 143, 163, 170, 185, 219, 229, 237, 276, 311, 320, 374; **29, 31, S.S.**
Clark, Kenneth, 16
Cortese, Cristoforo. *See* Manuscripts—Paris
Crane, Walter, 21, 23; **1**

Dali, Salvador, 23
Dargent, Yan, 22; **10, 11, 23, 24, 27, 34**
Delacroix, Eugene, 12, 19, 20, 24, 130, 163; **33, S.S.**
Divine Comedy, editions: 1481 (Florence), 16, **1, 2, 3, 9, 14, 16–19;** 1487 (Brescia), 16, 118, **7;** 1491, 16; 1493, 16; 1497, 16; 1506 (Florence), 16, **1;** 1544 (Venice), 16, 17, **frontis, chapter pages for all cantos, also 1, 4, 5, 8, 34;** 1555 (Venice), 16, **3, 34;** 1564 (Venice), 17; 1757 (Venice), 17, 19, **4, 8, 20, 24;** 1804, **33**
Doré, Gustave, 21, 22; **1, 4, 5, 7, 8, 10, 12, 13, 14, 17, 21, 23, 26, 28, 31, 32, 33, 34**

Editions of the *Divine Comedy*. See *Divine Comedy; see also* "Selected List of Illustrated Editions"

Eliot, T. S., 12, 13, 57, 87, 29

Fallani, Giovanni, 23
Fazzini, Pericle, 23; **13**
Feuerbach, Anselm, 19, 21, 47; **5**
Flaxman, John, 19, 20; **2, 3, 5, 6, 8, 15–18, 21, 23, 24, 27, 30, 31, 32, 34**
Florence. *See* Manuscripts—Florence
Fogg Museum (Harvard University). *See* Blake, William
Frescos. *See* Taddeo di Bartolo; Nardo di Cione; Giotto; Giovanni da Modena; Michelangelo; Luca Signorelli; Francesco Traini
Fruosino, Bartolomeo di, 12, 14, 15, 18, 22; **S.S.** *See also* Manuscripts—Paris
Fuseli, Henry, 19; **32, 33**

Genelli, Buonaventura, 20
Gericault, Theodore, 19, 20
Giotto (Last Judgement fresco, Arena Chapel, Padua), 11, 17, 276, 374; **S.S.**
Giraldi, Guglielmo. *See* Manuscripts—Vatican
Gosling, Nigel, 22
Greco, Aldo, 25; **3, 33**
Grosz, George, 23
Guttuso, Renato, 24, 25; **3, 18, 24, 32**

Holm, Ebba, 23; **7, 16, 20, 23, 27**

Imola. *See* Manuscripts—Imola

Koch, Joseph Anton, 20; **1, 2, 13, 16, 17, 18, 25**
Koch, T. W., 28
Kokoschka, Oscar, 19, 21, 23; **5**
Kraus, F. X., 28; **S.S.**
Kunz, Karl, 23

Lebrun Rico, 24, 25; **25, 28, 29**
Lippmann, F., 15, 16
Locella, Baron Guglielmo, 19, 87
London. *See* Manuscripts—London
Louvre Museum, Paris. *See* Delacroix, Eugene

Macchiavelli, Giovan, 20
Maintani, Lorenzo, 276; **24**
Mambelli, Giuliano, 28
Manfredini, Manfredo, 22; **1, 4, 5, 6, 7, 11, 13, 18, 22, 31, 33**
Manuscripts (illuminations or miniatures):
—Budapest: University Library, MS 33 (Venetian, ca. 1345), **3, 4**
—Chantilly: Musee Conde, MS 597 (Pisan, ca. 1345), 14, 15, 20; **3, 7, 16, 21, 25**
—Florence: Biblioteca Laurenziana, MS Plut. 40.1 (North Italian, 1456), **8, 16, 22**
—Florence: Biblioteca Laurenziana, MS Plut. 40.3 (Sienese, ca. 1345), **1**
—Florence: Biblioteca Nazionale, MS. B.R. 39 (Lombard, ca. 1400), **2, 32**
—Florence: Biblioteca Nazionale, MS. Palat. 313 (Florentine, ca. 1330s), 14; **15, 19, 20, 22**
—Florence: Biblioteca Riccardiana, MS. 1035 (Venetian, 2nd quarter XV cent.), **1**

—Imola: Biblioteca Comunale, MS. 32 (Lombard, ca. 1440, part of MS it. 2017, Paris, Bibliotheque Nationale), **11, 29**
—London: British Museum, Additional MS. 19587 (Neapolitan, ca. 1370), **2, 31**
—London: British Museum, Egerton MS 943 (Emilian or Paduan, 2nd quarter XIV cent.), **17, 23, 31**
—London: British Museum, Yates Thompson MS 36 (Priamo della Quercia, ca. 1442–50), 14, 15; **6, 8, 11, 14, 15, 32**
—Modena: Biblioteca Estense, MS R.4.8 (Emilian, early XV cent.), **29**
—Naples: Biblioteca Girolamini, MS C.F. 4.20 (Central or South Italian, 3rd quarter XIV cent.), **29**
—New York: The Pierpont Morgan Library, MS 676 (Italian, late XIV cent.), **9, 34**
—Padua: Biblioteca del Seminario, MS 67 (Paduan, early XV cent.), **6, 24**
—Paris: Bibliotheque Nationale, MS it. 74 (Florentine, Bartolomeo di Fruosino, ca. 1420), 12, 14, 15, 18, 22; **8, 10, 13, 14, 16, 17, 22, 23, 24, 25, 27, 30, S.S.**
—Paris: Bibliotheque Nationale, MS it. 78 (Cristoforo Cortese, 1st half XV cent.), **3, 8**
—Paris: Bibliotheque Nationale, MS it. 2017 (Lombard, ca. 1440, part of MS. Imola, Biblioteca Comunale, MS 32), 14, 15; **1, 5, 6, 12, 13, 18, 23, 31, 33**
—Rome: Biblioteca Angelica, MS 1102 (Bolognese, early XV cent.), 14; **21, 29**
—Vatican: Biblioteca Apostolica, MS lat. 4776 (Florentine, ca. 1390–1400), 12, 14, 15, 18; **1, 4, 5, 7, 9–20, 21, 22, 24–25, 26, 27, 28, 30, 32–33, 34**
—Vatican: Biblioteca Apostolica, MS Urb. lat. 365 (Guglielmo Giraldi and assistants, ca. 1478), 14, 15, 16; **3, 4, 9, 10, 12, 13, 15, 18, 34**
—Venice: Biblioteca Marciana, MS it. IX.276 (Venetian, late XIV cent.), 14, 22; **6**
Marko, Luïgi, **30**
Mazza, Emma, 23; **3, 14, 20**
Meiss, Millard, 11, 18, 118, S.S.
Michael, Meszaros, **6**
Michelangelo (Last Judgement fresco, Sistine Chapel, Vatican), 11, 12, 18, 20, 22, 24, 87; **S.S.**
Migneco, Giuseppe, **30**
Mirko, **29**
Modena. *See* Manuscripts—Modena
Modena, Giovanni da (Last Judgement fresco, San Petronio, Bologna), 17, 276, 374; **S.S.**
Morgan Library. *See* Manuscripts—New York
Moser, Barry, 24

Naples. *See* Manuscripts—Naples
National Gallery of Victoria. *See* Blake, William
New York City. *See* Manuscripts—New York

Orvieto, Duomo, bas-relief, 276; **24**. *See also* Maitani, Signorelli

Padua. *See* Giotto; Manuscripts—Padua
Paolo, Giovanni di, 17; **S.S.**
Paris. *See* Manuscripts—Paris
Phillips, Tom, 23

Pinelli, Bartolomeo, 20; **3, 5, 19, 26**
Pisa. *See* Traini; Manuscripts—Pisa
Pollard, A. W., 16
Pope-Hennessey, John, S.S.
Purificato, Domenico, 23; **6**

Quercia, Priamo della. *See* Manuscripts—London

Rauschenberg, Robert, 23
Reynolds, Joshua, 19, 359
Rodin, Auguste, 19, 21, 22; **5, 33**
Roe, Albert, 21, 37, 77, 87, 333, 346
Romano, Umberto, 23
Rome. *See* Manuscripts—Rome
Rossetti, Dante G., 19, 21, 47; **5**

Sabatelli, Luigi, **33**
San Gimignano. *See* Bartolo, Taddeo di
San Marco, Florence. *See* Angelico, Fra
Santa Maria Novella, Florence. *See* Cione, Nardo di
Santayana, George, 12, 13, 87
Sassu, Aligi, 25; **3, 27**
Scaramuzza, Francesco, 22, 23; **3, 7, 9, 14, 21, 31, 32, 33, 34**
Scheffer, Ary, 19; **5**
Siena. *See* Paolo, Giovanni di; Quercia, Priamo della

Signorelli, Luca (Inferno fresco, Cathedral, Orvieto), 11, 12, 15, 18, 22, 87; **S.S.**
Stassen, Franz, 23; **20, 25**
Stradanus, Giovanni (Jan van der Straet), 18; **1, 4, 7, 8, 16, 18, 33–34**

Tate Gallery, London. *See* Blake, William
Toynbee, Paget, 19
Traini, Francesco (Last Judgement, fresco, Camposanto, Pisa), 17, 107, 276, 374; **S.S.**

Uffizi Museum, Florence. *See* Zuccaro, Federico

Vasari, Giorgio, 17
Vatican. *See* Manuscripts—Vatican
Venice. *See* Manuscripts—Venice
Victoria, National Gallery of. *See* Blake, William
Volkmann, Ludwig, 11, 14, 15, 16, 17, 18, 20, 22, 23, 28, 170, S.S.

Watts, George Frederick, 19, 21; **5**

Yeats, William Butler, 21, 22

Zuccaro, Federico, 18; **3, 7, 9, 19, 27, 31**